# CARE & COUNSEL
## FOR
# COMBAT TRAUMA

## TRAINING PROGRAM WORKBOOK
## FOR AUDIT ONLY

Produced by
Light University,
American Association of Christian Counselors,
and the Military Ministry of Cru

**Care & Counsel for Combat Trauma Training Program Workbook For Audit Only**

Published by Cru Military, a division of Cru, 100 Lake Hart Drive, Orlando, FL 32832. For more information about Cru Military, please visit our web site at www. crumilitary.org.

DISCLAIMER

This book is not a substitute for appropriate medical or psychological care for those experiencing significant emotional pain or whose ability to function at home, school, or work is impaired.

Chronic or extreme stress may cause a wide assortment of physical and psychological problems. Some may require evaluation and treatment by medical or mental health professionals. When in doubt, seek advice from a professional.

ISBN: 978-0-9863630-8-5

# CARE & COUNSEL FOR COMBAT TRAUMA TRAINING PROGRAM WORKBOOK
## FOR AUDIT ONLY

**IMPORTANT: This workbook is only for those who wish to audit the Care & Counsel for Combat Trauma course and who do not need or want the Certificate of Completion.**

It is used in conjunction with the *CCCT Video Training Package available o*nline at www.crumilitary.org/ccct.

## Who Should Take This Course?

The Care & Counsel for Combat Trauma (CCCT) course is suitable for anyone with an interest in the effects of Combat Trauma and Post-Traumatic Stress Disorder (PTSD) and is particularly relevant for:

- Military and hospital chaplains
- Mental health professionals
- College/university counselors to veterans
- Emergency service personnel
- Rescue workers
- Pastors and ministry leaders
- Support group leaders/facilitators
- Health care personnel
- Anyone affected by combat trauma
- Family, friends, colleagues of sufferers
- Those living with the aftermath of combat experiences

## Entry Qualifications

There are no special requirements or background needed to enroll in or benefit from this course.

## Course Objectives

1. The CCCT Course will help you to develop a greater understanding of the complexities surrounding the post-combat experience of hundreds of thousands of active duty military members and veterans.

2. The CCCT Course will broaden professional and ministry-based skills.

3. The CCCT Course will equip Christian pastors and lay ministers to reach out with sensitivity and relevance to military members, veterans, and families in their congregations and communities.

# CARE & COUNSEL FOR COMBAT TRAUMA

## TABLE OF CONTENTS

# UNIT FOUR
# MILITARY APPLICATIONS                                          **141**

# UNIT FIVE
# SPIRITUAL SOLUTIONS                                            **183**

# BEFORE YOU BEGIN

Welcome to the *Care & Counsel for Combat Trauma* program of study. We believe you will find this program to be academically sound, clinically excellent, and biblically-based.

Our faculty represents some of the best in their field – including professors, counselors and ministers who provide students with current, practical instruction relevant to the needs of today's generations.

We have also worked hard to provide you with a program that is convenient and flexible – giving you the advantage of video-based "classroom instruction" while allowing you to complete your training on your own time and schedule within the comfort of your home or office.

**This "audit" version of the workbook does not include the exams or answer sheets required to receive a completion certificate.** Thank you for *daring to care* by enrolling in the *Care & Counsel for Combat Trauma* program. May you increase your knowledge and people-skills as you begin your study.

# MINISTERING TO THE MILITARY

As you work through *Care & Counsel for Combat Trauma*, consider how you can share hope and healing with our returning warriors, veterans and their families through a church-based or personal ministry. You can find more information about ministering to the military at www.crumilitary.org.

May God richly bless you as you pray and ponder how you can make a difference to a Soldier, Sailor, Airman, Marine or Coast Guardsman who has sacrificed selflessly for us.

*If not you, who? If not now, when?*

# UNIT ONE
# ACUTE STRESS AND TRAUMA

cru
MILITARY

MILITARY
MINISTRY

LightUniversity
Caring for People God's Way

# CCCT 101
# INTRODUCTION TO CRISIS COUNSELING
## Tim Clinton, Ed.D., MG (Ret.) Bob Dees,
## & Diane Langberg, Ph.D.

## Course Description

This lesson provides basic definitions of terms that students will be discussing throughout the entire course; provides reference points and statistics regarding trauma; and gives an overview of healing points showing how God is the ultimate antidote to trauma in a person's life. Since the church is called to minister to those who are suffering, this program will help educate and train leaders to respond to others in crisis.

## Learning Objectives

By the end of this lesson, students:

1. Will be able to apply relevant Scriptures to the issues of crisis and trauma.

2. Will be able to learn the definitions of crisis and trauma, and how this applies practically to the lives of people they Will be helping.

3. Will be able to understand key statistics and their importance regarding crisis intervention in victims suffering from trauma.

## I. Scriptures

**A.** Job 5:7 – *"But man is born to trouble as the sparks fly upward."*

**B.** Job 14:1 – *"Man who is born of a woman is few of days and full of trouble."*

**C.** John 16:33 – *" I have said these things to you, that in Me you may have peace. In the world you will have tribulation. But take heart; I have overcome the world."*

**D.** 1 John 5:19-20 – *"We know that we are from God, and the whole world lies in the power of the evil one. And we know that the Son of God has come and has given us understanding, so that we may know Him who is true; and we are in Him who is true, in His Son Jesus Christ. He is the true God and eternal life."*

## II. Crisis and Trauma

### A. Crisis – an event in life that is predictable or anticipated

- Life is full of ups and downs, but people will sometimes hit walls. Their ability to work their way through that challenging issue is everything. If they can't, disequilibrium or chaos occurs.

- Chinese symbol for crisis: Danger and Opportunity. "Threat clears a man's head." Threat causes people to examine danger but also provides the opportunity to change their course of action, which can be a healthy relationship between danger and opportunity.

- Coping skills: If they don't work, then panic can occur. It is dangerous if one cannot resolve the issue; opportunity occurs because it is at this point that one is most open to change, e.g., new ways of thinking or new values.

- Crisis causes self-reflection. Crisis is actually an opportunity for clarity; people can "get bitter or get better." It reveals a person's character. People can become aware of things in themselves that they are not happy about, but that they can now actually make the choice to change.

B. **Trauma – an event outside normal human experiences**

- It often causes feelings of powerlessness and hopelessness. Because the event is considered abnormal and outside of human experience, powerlessness is a key characteristic of a person's experience of trauma.

- The event causing trauma is abnormal; it differs from a crisis in that a person cannot use coping skills; there is nothing one can do to stop the event from happening.

- People will respond in completely different ways, even if they are trained the same. Even if two people experience the same event, their reactions may be completely different, and this is important to take into consideration.

- When violated, people can lose their sense of safety and security regarding other people, or even God Himself. People often think that the world shouldn't be the way they just experienced through that trauma, so they experience a horrific sense of a loss of safety. This causes a sense of isolation.

C. **Examples of Traumatic Events**

- Natural disasters (hurricanes, floods, tornadoes, etc.)

- Accidental disasters (car crashes, plane crashes, explosions, etc.)

- Intentional or deliberate disasters (bombings, robberies, suicides, rape, terrorism, hostage situations, etc.)

- Sustained or repeated events (war, kidnapping, sexual abuse, terrorist threats, spousal abuse, etc.)

# III. Statistics

A. **There are 400,000 untreated cases of PTSD from previous wars.**

B. **One in five Iraq and Afghanistan veterans suffers from PTSD or major depression.**

C. **It is thought that 70% of homeless veterans have major issues with PTSD.**

D. One in three women and one in five men are sexually abused prior to age 18 by someone they are supposed to love and trust, and many of the abuses are chronic.

E. One in four women in America experience rape during their lifetime.

F. 30% of women experience domestic violence at the hands of a husband or partner.

G. Women are twice as likely to experience PTSD than men are. This could be because women are not as capable of compartmentalizing as men are.

H. About 5.2 million U.S. adults ages 18-54 have PTSD in a given year.

I. 61% of men and 51% of women have experienced traumas linked to PTSD.

## IV. How a Crisis or Trauma Affects People

A. Trauma can teach a grossly unhealthy way of relating to God and other people.

B. Someone who experiences trauma is facing intrusive re-experiencing of the event.

C. Hyper-arousal – a loud boom; for example, fireworks could arouse extreme reactions in a veteran of war.

D. Numbing – Affect is flat.

E. Fight or Flight – In a situation perceived as dangerous, one either puts up a fight or runs away.

F. Dissociation – The mind takes a person someplace else other than the present in order to escape trauma.

G. Survivor Guilt – When others died, but a person survived. Forgiveness is the antidote to this.

H. Addiction – Self-medicating unresolved trauma.

I. What determines the type of impact and duration of impact on the person?

- Frequency

- Intensity

- Age

- Previous Trauma

- Help Given

J. PTSD is a normal human response to an abnormal situation.

K. Post-traumatic Growth – "Trauma can lead to positive change, improve relationships, the possibilities for one's life, a greater appreciation for life, a greater sense of personal strength and spiritual development … [there is] a basic paradox achieved by trauma survivors, that somewhere in the way, they now see their losses as producing valuable gains for them. They may find themselves becoming more comfortable with intimacy and having a greater sense of compassion for others who experience life difficulties." (Lawrence Calhoun and Richard Tedeschi, professors at UNC-Charlotte)

## V. Healing Grace

A. Psalm 46:1 – *"God is our refuge and strength, a very present help in trouble."*

B. Psalm 46:10 – *"Be still, and know that I am God. I will be exalted among the nations, I will be exalted in the earth!"*

C. Psalm 91:1, 4 – *"He who dwells in the shelter of the Most High will abide in the shadow of the Almighty ... He will cover you with His pinions, and under His wings you will find refuge; His faithfulness is a shield and buckler."*

D. Isaiah 45:3 – *"I will give you the treasures of darkness and the hoards in secret places, that you may know that it is I, the Lord, the God of Israel, who call you by your name."*

E. Though this is a difficult area, there is a great message of hope.

## CCCT 101 Study Questions

1. Discuss the implications of the Chinese symbol that represents "danger and opportunity," and why this is important when dealing with issues regarding crisis intervention.

2. Why would a person who has experienced trauma in life be dealing with feelings of powerlessness and hopelessness?

3. What are the four categories of traumatic events?

4. According to the Department of Veterans Affairs, how many untreated cases of PTSD are there from previous wars in the United States today, causing a "national epidemic"?

5. What is post-traumatic growth, and why is this important to understand when dealing with symptoms of post-traumatic stress?

# CCCT 102
# GRIEF, LOSS, AND COMPLICATED GRIEF
## Eric Scalise, Ph.D.

## Course Description

Grief can only be experienced when there has been a loss of an intimate relationship or an object of concern or affection. People grieve because they love; and unfortunately, love and life can hurt. If people refuse to deal with grief and traumatic events, they will withdraw from life and only exist in emotional exile and never be able to benefit from the joys of human experience. Rarely are there easy answers when people experience tragic kinds of losses that are often untimely. However, there is a message of hope, and God can use people to convey that message to a world that is hurting.

## Learning Objectives

By the end of this lesson, students:

1. Will be able to learn the nature and consequences of stress, as well as factors that might help determine the intensity, severity, and duration of a grief response.

2. Will be able to understand the grief cycle and its stages.

3. Will be able to understand complicated grief and how it differs from normal grief and loss.

## I. The Nature and Consequences of Stress

A. Grieving is a normal response to loss, and often includes feelings of intense sorrow, anger, depression, loneliness, and possible physical symptoms.

B. Grief is oftentimes crisis-oriented. The crisis can be real, anticipated, and/or imagined; however, the impact can be the same.

C. Grief is universal, but how a person walks through grief is individual. C.S. Lewis said, "God whispers to us in our pleasures, speaks to us in our conscience, but shouts in our pains: it is His megaphone to rouse a deaf world."

## II. Factors That Might Help Determine the Intensity, Severity, and Duration of a Grief Response

A. Intensity (the strength of feelings and dynamics)

B. Severity (often individualized)

C. Duration

- Type of loss

- Prior knowledge and anticipation

- Lack of support system

- Personal belief system

## III. Grief Cycle

A. Shock (Initial paralysis that comes as soon as a person becomes aware the event has taken place)

B. Denial (As soon as the shock hits, people are often trying to avoid the inevitable reality of what that means. It is easier to say, "It can't be so.")

C. Anger (Release of all the overwhelming emotions that might be bottled up; trying to push it away. People may go through an explosive release.)

D. Bargaining (Seeking in vain to find a way out of the crisis and trying to bargain out of the reality. Believers often try to bargain with God.)

E. Depression (Final realization of the inevitable reality of that loss or event in life)

F. Testing (Person learns, though accepted reality, how to go on in life.)

G. Acceptance (Person finally discovers a way out of that place and can move on in life.)

## IV. Complicated Grief

A. Complicated grief occurs when a person becomes stuck and struggles to break free from the powerful grip of traumatic circumstances.

B. Complicated grief is an extreme version of normal grief, and it can sometimes mimic PTSD. Some examples of this include the symptoms of survivor guilt, extreme agitation, depressive episodes, suicidal ideation, very intense sensitivity to most things that would stimulate a person, and intrusive thoughts.

C. Someone experiencing complicated grief could have great coping skills, but complicated grief is more connected to the original relationship with a person, object, or some process that is going on. A person could experience difficulty speaking about the event, constantly bringing up themes of death and loss in casual conversations, sleep and appetite disturbance, self-destructive behaviors, excessive avoidance and isolation, significant impairment in normal areas of functioning, and very strong reactions to triggers in normal events.

D. Approximately 10-20% of people who experience significant loss are at risk of developing complicated grief.

## V. Dynamics That Contribute to Complicated Grief

A. The mode of the loss was incomprehensible.

B. The loss is considered exceptionally untimely.

C. There is a sense of survival guilt.

D. Their culture or environment disallows the grief process.

E. There is an excessive attachment and proximity to the deceased person's possessions.

F. Normal activities are resumed without allowing for normal grief.

## VI. Ministry Opportunities: Acts 3:1-11

A. Acts 3:1-11 gives a biblical example of working with people who experience grief and loss. The beggar had experienced the loss of physical ability, the ability to earn income, certain social status within culture, as well as independence and freedom. He was truly in need.

B. The first thing Peter and John gave the beggar was a sense of worth by giving their time and attention, by not judging, and by inviting him to join in what God was doing.

C. The second thing Peter and John gave the beggar was a reason to hope by creating some expectancy, by commanding attention, and by building faith.

D. The third thing Peter and John gave the beggar was real help by being involved, by being practical, and by being genuinely authentic.

E. The fourth thing Peter and John gave the beggar was an introduction to Jesus by acknowledging His name, by acknowledging His deity, and lastly, by acknowledging His humanity.

F. The fifth thing Peter and John gave the beggar was a sense of belonging by accepting him where he was, leading him in a new direction, and changing his life script (from lame, begging, and outside the house of God, to whole, belonging, and inside the house of God). When people experience tragic grief, their lives as they knew them are shattered. This loss and grief may usher in the end of a chapter, but not the end of the story.

G. The sixth thing Peter and John gave the beggar was the opportunity to be a witness by being visible and present, by confirming the impossible, and by drawing the hungry.

## VII. Conclusion

Be a healing bridge to a community that is hurting, both within the church and within the community and beyond. God can use people to touch those who have been impacted by tragedy, grief, and loss. Be sensitive to point out the way, to show that there are answers, and to show that believers serve a God of hope, and that hope is Christ, who is the Hope of Glory.

## CCCT 102 Study Questions

1. List and discuss the different factors that might help determine the intensity, severity, and duration of a grief response.

2. What are the stages of the grief cycle, and why are they important to understand?

3. What are some similarities between physical symptoms of complicated grief and physical symptoms of PTSD?

4. What are some of the dynamics that can contribute to complicated grief within a person who has just experienced a tragic loss in his/her life?

5. Discuss the six things Peter and John gave the beggar in the Acts 3:1-11 passage discussed by Dr. Scalise in the presentation.

# CCCT 103
# TRAUMA AND ABUSE
## Diane Langberg, Ph.D.

## Course Description

Abuse has become more prominent in the United States, which indicates that the term "abuse" has been overused and misapplied at times. This undermines the reality and profound negative impact that abuse has on individuals and their relationships. Dr. Langberg will address sources of abuse, general responses to abuse, and normal trauma response patterns.

## Learning Objectives

By the end of this lesson, students:

1. Will be able to be familiar with the different types of abuse that occur in the United States today.

2. Will be able to understand the impact that abuse has on the lives of the victims.

3. Will be able to learn how Christians can respond to those victims in a healing way.

# I. Types of Abuse

## A. Physical Abuse – using physical power to control, manipulate, or intimidate another person.

- Between 25 and 30% of male and female children suffer physical abuse.

- 31% of adult women in the United States will experience one episode of violence at the hands of a husband or partner.

- More than three women are murdered daily by husbands or partners.

- Pregnant women are more likely to be victims of homicide than to die from any other cause.

- Physical abuse can occur and be terrifying, oppressive, and damaging even when physical evidence is not on the body.

## B. Verbal Abuse – using verbal power to control, manipulate, or intimidate another person.

## C. Emotional Abuse – the systematic tearing down of another human being by rejecting, ignoring, terrorizing, isolating, or corrupting them.

- It is also the use of emotional power in a relationship to control, manipulate, or intimidate another person.

- Emotional abuse is often more subtle, and often accompanies physical or verbal abuse.

## D. Spiritual Abuse – the use of spiritual power, position, or information to control, intimidate or manipulate another person.

- Always involves a distortion of the word of God

- Always involves a distortion of the character of God

E. **Sexual Abuse – any sexual activity – visual, verbal, or physical – engaged in without consent.**

- A child is never considered able to consent.

- Most sexual abuse of children is perpetrated by a family member or someone known to the child.

- In the United States, there are about 80,000 reported incidents of child sexual abuse each year.

- One in five girls report being solicited for sex on the Internet prior to the age of 18.

- 20% of men in the United States report being sexually abused prior to the age of 18.

- At least 20% of women and 12% of adolescent girls have experienced sexual assault or rape during their lifetimes.

- About 700,000 women are sexually assaulted each year in the United States, which equivocates to more than one per minute.

- Close to 100,000 men are raped each year.

- Two-thirds of rape victims had a prior relationship to their offender.

- 70% of reported assaults are committed against victims 17 years of age or younger.

- Between 50 and 85% of American females will experience some sort of sexual harassment during their academic or working lives.

F. **Rape – non-consensual sexual penetration obtained by physical force, by threat of bodily harm, or at a time when the victim is incapable of giving consent due to mental illness, mental retardation, or intoxication of some kind.**

G. **Sexual Harassment – any action occurring within the workplace whereby one person is treated as the object of another's sexual prerogative.**

## II. The Impact of Abuse

### A. Duration, frequency, and intensity all affect the impact of trauma.

- Untreated abuse can result in somatic problems.

- Abuse of children causes stress that can disrupt early brain development and development of the nervous and immune systems.

- Repeated abuse can teach a victim to "turn off" his/her emotions.

- Problems stemming from abuse can impact relationships.

### B. A Trauma Reaction to Abuse

- There is an ongoing re-experiencing of the trauma.

- There is a numbing of responsiveness.

- There are ongoing increased arousal symptoms.

### C. To be a victim means to be someone who has suffered from an injurious action.

### D. To be a survivor means to be someone who has continued to function and learned how to prosper in spite of abuse.

## III. How Can Christian Helpers Respond to Those Who Have Been Abused So That They Are Helped and Transformed?

**Learn from the Lord:**

### A. They must first leave glory.

### B. They must "become little."

### C. They must enter darkness.

D. They must bear the character of the Father, full of Grace and Truth.

E. They must not abandon those in need.

F. They must not lose perspective and allow their thinking to be distorted.

## IV. Conclusion

A. Isaiah 45:2-3 – *"I will go before you and level the exalted places, I will break in pieces the doors of bronze and cut through the bars of iron, I will give you the treasures of darkness and the hoards in secret places, that you may know that it is I, the Lord, the God of Israel, who call you by your name."*

B. When one part of the body suffers, the entire body is affected. Suffering limits how life is lived.

C. The body of Christ must choose to be a sanctuary for the abused.

## CCCT 103 Study Questions

1. Discuss the similarities and the differences of physical, verbal, emotional, spiritual, and sexual abuse.

2. Discuss children regarding sexual abuse. Why would they never be considered able to consent?

3. According to Dr. Langberg, duration, frequency, and intensity all affect the impact of trauma. Discuss these three factors regarding how each factor would impact a victim of abuse.

4. What are some of the spiritual implications of abuse that a victim may face?

5. Discuss the ways that Christian helpers can learn from the Lord in how to help victims of abuse obtain healing in their lives.

# CCCT 104
# ANXIETY AND DEPRESSION
## Archibald Hart, Ph.D.

## Course Description

This lesson will focus on how Post-Traumatic Stress Disorder (PTSD) creates anxiety and depression. Dr. Hart will discuss definitions of terms, the prevalence of different types of trauma, risk signs, significant statistics, and prevention and intervention strategies that helpers can utilize. Students will learn the connection between PTSD and anxiety and depression problems, and they will become more educated on how those problems can be prevented and/or treated.

## Learning Objectives

By the end of this lesson, students:

1. Will be able to understand how trauma, stress, and depression/anxiety relate in sufferers of PTSD.

2. Will be able to understand what it is about trauma that puts people at risk for developing depression and/or anxiety problems.

3. Will be able to learn prevention and intervention strategies regarding the depression and anxiety components of PTSD.

## I. How Do Trauma, Stress, and Depression Relate?

A. PTSD, depression, and anxiety disorder frequently follow traumatic exposure – both separately and concurrently.

B. In the immediate aftermath (acute PTSD), they appear to be separate disorders.

C. In chronic PTSD, they become comorbid.

## II. Prevalence of Types of Trauma

A. Assault – 38%

B. Serious Car Accidents – 28%

C. Other Accidents or Injury – 14%

D. Fire, Flood, Earthquakes – 17%

E. Life-Threatening Illness – 5%

F. Sudden Death of Friend/Family Member – 60%

G. Learning About Others' Trauma – 60%

H. War – ???

## III. Risks of Developing Depression/Anxiety Problems Following PTSD

A. Traumatic stress is far more powerful and serious than ordinary day-to-day stress.

B. PTSD sufferers experience twice the risk for major depression and anxiety disorders.

C. Preexisting depression and traumatic childhood memories are two risk factors that will exacerbate the effects of trauma.

## IV. Anxiety Orders Triggered by PTSD

A. Panic Attacks

B. Agoraphobia

C. Other Phobias

D. Obsessive-Compulsive Disorder

E. General Anxiety Disorders

F. Separation Anxiety

## V. Depression Disorders Triggered by PTSD

A. Major Depression

B. Unstable Mood Disorder

C. Bipolar Disorder/Manic Episodes

# VI. Definitions

    A. **Endogenous Anxiety or Depression** – Anxiety or depression "from within" which is primarily biochemical

    B. **Exogenous Anxiety or Depression** – Anxiety or depression "from without" which is brought on due to life circumstances

# VII. Neurobiology of Mood Disorders

    A. **The Trauma Triangle**

- Prefrontal cortex – orchestrates thoughts and actions with internal goals; takes control of emotions

- Amygdala – primary role in the processing and memory of emotional reactions, especially fear

- Hippocampus – vital to emotional arousal and the formation of long-term memories

    B. **Cortisol**

- One of the stress hormones released by the adrenal system

- The surge of cortisol creates the effects in the Trauma Triangle that then lead to depression or anxiety.

# VIII. Statistics

    A. **Major Depression and PTSD occur together early on after the trauma in 30% (PTSD at one month).**

    B. **17.5% had PTSD at four months.**

    C. **45% of PTSD patients had comorbid depression at four months.**

    D. **When depression and PTSD are comorbid, symptom severity was more severe overall. They interact to increase distress.**

## IX. Risk Factors

### A. Risk Factors for Developing Serious Depression and Anxiety Following Trauma

- Preexisting morbidity

- Lack of social/environmental support

- Prolongation of traumatic stress

- Lack of coping skills, helplessness

- Antisocial or borderline personality traits

### B. Suicide Risk in PTSD-related Depression

- Among combat soldiers, suicide rate is the highest it has ever been.

- Suicide is seen as a coping mechanism.

- Risk Factors:

  1) male

  2) alcohol use

  3) abuse

  4) family history of suicide

  5) poor social environment

  6) history of attempting suicide

- Combat Trauma Risk Factors

  1) multiple wounding

  2) extreme guilt reaction

  3) loss of close friend

  4) sense of hopelessness

## X. Clinical Intervention

### A. Reduce the Cortisol Stress Response

### B. Long-term SSRI's to Counter Hippocampal Atrophy

### C. Cognitive Behavioral Therapy

### D. Relaxation and Meditation

### E. Targeted Family Interventions

## CCCT 104 Study Questions

1. Discuss the different types of trauma and their prevalence. Are any of these surprising; if so, which ones?

2. What are some factors that could worsen trauma within a sufferer of PTSD?

3. Define "endogenous anxiety or depression" and "exogenous anxiety or depression." Why is understanding these definitions important when examining people displaying symptoms of PTSD?

4. Discuss the Trauma Triangle and the importance of the prefrontal cortex, the amygdala, and the hippocampus.

5. Discuss the clinical and biblical interventions that were mentioned by Dr. Hart.

# CCCT 105
# TRAUMA AND ATTACHMENT
## Gary Sibcy, Ph.D.

## Course Description

In this lesson, Dr. Sibcy discusses the attachment theory and how it relates to trauma. Attachment is a theory of relationships and emotion, with safety being a key component in understanding problems. Dr. Sibcy will teach students how to apply the attachment theory to trauma situations, and students will learn to better understand the correlation between trauma and how people do relationships.

## Learning Objectives

By the end of this lesson, students:

1. Will be able to understand the five components of the attachment system.

2. Will be able to understand the four attachment styles that people can have, and what each of the styles mean regarding how people act in relationships.

3. Will be able to learn how attachment styles relate to trauma, PTSD, as well as understanding the components of effective therapies counselors can utilize.

## I. What is Attachment?

A. Attachment is a theory of relationships and emotion, where safety is a key component in understanding problems.

B. Affect Regulation – how people learn to deal with their deepest and strongest emotions.

C. Two sets of beliefs develop from interactions with the attachment figure: beliefs about self and beliefs about others.

## II. Five Components of the Attachment System

A. A caregiver's response to a child in distress affects that child's underlying beliefs about trust.

B. A caregiver is a "secure base" or "safe haven" for a child.

C. Secure Base Phenomena – when children feel calm and secure, they feel free to explore the world.

D. Separation leads to anxiety and anger.

E. Loss of attachment figure leads to intense grief and a sense of not wanting to move on.

## III. Four Attachment Styles

A. Secure Attachment – positive view of self; positive view of others

B. Dismissing/Avoidant Attachment – overly positive view of self; overly negative view of others

C. Preoccupied Attachment – overly negative view of self; overly positive view of others

D. Disorganized/Fearful Attachment – negative view of self; negative view of others

## IV. PTSD, Trauma, and Attachment

A. What is PTSD?

- Exposure to a life-threatening event

- Intense emotional reaction to the event

- Re-experiencing of the event

- Avoidance of anything that could trigger the emotional response experienced during the event

- Hyperarousal or hyperstartle tendencies

B. It is important to understand that not everyone exposed to a traumatic event will develop PTSD.

C. Natural Recovery

- Re-exposure to stressful events will activate stress.

- When the negative expectation doesn't happen, there is a disparity which causes anxiety to naturally extinguish itself.

- With repeated practice, anxiety may leave entirely.

D. PTSD & Other Anxiety Disorders

- Re-exposure to stressful events over-activates the emotional system.

- There is no experience of disparity due to avoidance strategies.

- Unhealthy tension-reduction strategies may be used to calm their emotional systems.

E. **Components of Effective Therapies**

- Employ titrated exposure.

- Create disparity to bring about healing.

- Use cognitive interventions to help change negative thinking patterns.

- Work on affect regulation strategies.

- Deal with "relatedness" issues.

F. **Attachment and the Counselor**

- Therapeutic Window – creating enough stress – but not too much stress – so that disparity can be experienced.

- Individuals with avoidant attachment are more likely to have difficulty using you as a secure base.

- Preoccupied individuals tend to be overwhelmed, and they are very demanding and sensitive.

- A disorganized attachment style may give a very inconsistent pattern of responding to the counselor.

## V.  Attachment, PTSD, and the Family

A. **The anger and irritability common to PTSD can be very traumatic to the family.**

B. **Children who have a parent with PTSD live life "on edge."**

C. PTSD survivors struggle with a deep sense of hollowness and emptiness. Family members experience this emotional detachment as coldness and rejection.

D. Happy Phobia – the brain equates positive emotions with vulnerability in an attempt to avoid unexpected trauma.

**CCCT 105 Study Questions**

1. Describe the attachment theory in general, and how it is important in understanding people and their relationships.

2. What are the five components of the attachment system?

3. Discuss the four attachment styles taught in the video, and compare and contrast how these different attachment styles affect relationships.

4. What components are required for a person to be considered to have PTSD?

5. Discuss the components of effective therapies, and why each of these would be useful when counseling people suffering from trauma.

# CCCT 106
# COUNSELING STRATEGIES PANEL
## Eric Scalise, Ph.D., Jennifer Cisney, M.A., & Kevin Ellers, D.Min.

## Course Description

> This lesson, led by an expert panel, will expose students to counseling strategies regarding trauma survivors. Dr. Scalise, Jennifer Cisney, and Dr. Ellers will explain different models of counseling that can be used with trauma survivors, indications and contraindications related to caregiving, the importance of a multidisciplinary intervention approach, and the need for support systems. Finally, the panel will discuss the recovery process with a biblical model of healing and restoration.

## Learning Objectives

By the end of this lesson, students:

1. Will be able to learn the characteristics of acute care, and how psychological first aid differs from psychotherapy.

2. Will be able to learn the contraindications of acute care, and when a person needs immediate mental health intervention.

3. Will be able to learn how to structure a community team that is multidisciplinary, as well as what the role of the church can be regarding crisis intervention strategies.

## I. Acute Trauma and Stress

A. The initial response to a crisis is not psychotherapy.

B. Psychological First Aid – Immediate response that can be performed by anyone who is trained.

C. Characteristics of Acute Care

- Supportive

- Stabilizing

- Practical

D. In a crisis, people aren't processing information, but rather they are feeling information.

E. Crisis responders can help alleviate acute stress by giving information to help them understand why they are feeling and experiencing what they are.

F. Who needs acute care and who doesn't?

- Psychological triage is extremely important.

- For example, a little bit of confusion following trauma is normal. However, not being in touch with reality requires intervention.

- Suicidal ideation, extreme anger or violence, self-destructive behaviors, or anything that can be of immediate danger to the person needs to be addressed immediately.

G. What are the contraindications of acute care?

- Homicidal, suicidal, psychotic, loss of touch with reality – any of these behaviors require mental health care.

- Sometimes when a crisis comes up on someone who already has a preexisting issue he/she is struggling with, the normal coping mechanisms are not just overwhelmed, but are completely shut down.

- If someone cannot be stabilized, he/she will need immediate mental health intervention.

**H. Strategies to Deal with Immediate Grief if Someone is Facing a Loss**

- Come to terms with the reality of what's happened

- Note: Debriefings are only done in a group setting. Crisis interventions may be done one on one.

# II. Multidisciplinary Approach

**A. Churches can create community teams for crisis intervention.**

**B. A multidisciplinary team would have mental health professionals, clergy, peers, and people who have had losses/trauma themselves.**

**C. Empower the locals to form community teams and have local resources. People often show up at the beginning but then are gone. A person's crisis may hit months later, not during the acute stage.**

# III. Role of the Church After the Trauma

**A. Be a long-term support system.**

**B. Some symptoms are normal responses, but how, when, and to what level people experience those symptoms will vary from person to person.**

**C. The Role Changes: The long-term role of the church shapes the way people integrate the traumatic experience in their lives whether in a positive or negative way. This can be critical for people when they are putting their lives back together.**

D. The church should be there for people as they process cognitively.

E. People need to have the freedom and space to process what happened.

F. People need to have time to calm themselves in order to quiet themselves and calm their system down, being careful not to isolate themselves from others.

## IV. Good Intentions vs. Good Results

A. It is very important to be trained in crisis intervention.

B. Some people make the mistake of trying to fix something, when people really need a loving presence.

C. The Holy Spirit's presence in the responder's life can speak volumes to a person in crisis.

D. Be discerning and wise.

E. Provide a safe, loving environment where people can talk.

F. Be a safe person who is not afraid of others' pain.

G. Believers engaging people in crisis or trauma must understand that the people in crisis are often having a crisis of faith.

H. Do this work oneself and know one's own theology of suffering. Believers have the hope of Christ – He can heal the pain and transform the person.

## V.   Conclusion

A.  Important counseling strategies include being there in the moment, not doing lots of cognitive work, psychological triage, priortization, understanding the process, having a team approach that is multidisciplinary, and having the church offer long-term community support and care.

B.  Crisis intervention is not as much about doing as it is about being.

C.  Crisis intervention is one of the toughest ministries to be a part of, because the helper will be walking through some of people's darkest times. If one chooses to do so, he/she will have the blessing and honor of being there for someone when he/she is most open to God's transformative power.

D.  People are not human *doings*; they are human beings. The value of presence is what Christ calls believers to.

E.  It is a sacred trust to engage with people at their moment of crisis and need, and believers have the opportunity to be the body of Christ on this earth.

**CCCT 106 Study Questions**

1. Discuss the characteristics of acute care and how it differs from traditional psychotherapy.

2. What is psychological triage?

3. Discuss the contraindications of acute care and when it might be necessary to refer a person for mental health intervention.

4. What are the advantages of having a multidisciplinary community team when engaging in crisis intervention?

5. Discuss the role of the church after trauma, and why it is important to a local community to have the support of the church.

# UNIT TWO
# BASIC CRISIS INTERVENTION

cru
MILITARY

MILITARY
MINISTRY

LightUniversity
Caring for People God's Way

# CCCT 201
# IMPACT DYNAMICS OF CRISIS AND TRAUMA
Jennifer Cisney, M.A.

## Course Description

In this lesson, Jennifer Cisney will define psychological first aid in crisis intervention and discuss the impact of crisis and trauma on the individual in a broad context. Furthermore, students will become familiar with the various ways people battle symptoms. Students will learn the first steps regarding assessment tools and protocols in responding to someone in crisis and trauma situations.

## Learning Objectives

By the end of this lesson, students:

1. Will be able to learn the history and background of crisis intervention, basic definitions, and the importance of crisis intervention by studying a broader context.

2. Will be able to understand the general, emotional, behavioral, physical, and spiritual symptoms of post-traumatic stress.

3. Will be able to learn basic principles regarding the first steps in responding to people in crisis.

## I. Background of Crisis Intervention

**A. Crisis intervention is a relatively new field, and modern-day crisis intervention has its roots in the military.**

**B. Studies show that early intervention reduces chronic psychiatric morbidity.**

**C. Dynamics of Modern Crisis Intervention**

- Immediacy

- Proximity

- Expectancy

**D. Definitions**

- Critical Incident – the catalyst for emotional or psychological trauma

- Crisis – the reaction of the individual to the incident that has occurred

- Crisis Intervention – the application of "psychological first aid"

**E. Psychological First Aid**

- Stabilize people of their symptoms

- Symptom reduction

- Reestablish a functional capacity

- Seek a higher level of care

**F. "While most survivors of violence and mass disaster will recover normally from their psychological post-traumatic stress, it is important to do early psychological interventions to those who are in need. The interventions should be phasic multi-component integrated intervention systems." (Mental Health and Mass Violence Report, 2002, NIMH)**

## G. Consider Follow-Up Services For:

- The bereaved

- Those with preexisting psychiatric disorders

- Those requiring medical surgical intervention

- Those with Acute Stress Disorder

- Those with chronic or intense exposure

- Those who request additional care

## H. Broader Context

- 90% of U.S. citizens will be exposed to a traumatic event in their lifetime. Of those, 13% of females and 6% of males will develop PTSD.

- Crisis intervention seeks to prevent the onset of PTSD.

- Suicide following traumatic events

    1) 63% increase in first year after an earthquake

    2) 31% increase in first two years after a hurricane

    3) 14% increase four years after a flood

- U.S. citizens aged 12 or older experienced 37 million crimes in 1996.

- Each year, approximately one million people become victims of violent crime while at work.

- In 1994, U.S. hospital emergency rooms treated approximately 1.4 million injuries resulting from interpersonal acts of violence.

- In 1997, there were 304 acts of international terrorism with one-third directed at U.S. targets.

- Among urban U.S. firefighters, almost 32% were assessed with symptoms consistent with a diagnosis of PTSD.

## II. Signs and Symptoms

A. Post-traumatic stress is actually a helpful mechanism, created by God, as a response to threats of safety.

B. In the crisis moment, the frontal lobe of the brain becomes disabled, and decision-making is handled by the amygdala.

C. In the crisis moment, blood flow is redirected from vital organs to the muscles to increase physical strength.

D. In the crisis moment, awareness of pain is lessened.

E. Post-traumatic stress is the normal reaction to an abnormal event.

F. General Symptoms of Post-Traumatic Stress

- Confusion and an inability to concentrate

- Difficulty making decisions

- Sensory distortions

- Inappropriate guilt and regret

- Preoccupation with the event

- Inability to understand the consequences of their behavior

- Psychosis and loss of touch with reality

G. Emotional Symptoms of Post-Traumatic Stress

- High levels of anxiety and irritability

- Inappropriate levels of anger

- Panic

- Vegetative depression

- Extreme fear, phobia

- Extreme grief

**H. Behavioral Symptoms of Post-Traumatic Stress**

- Impulsiveness and risk taking

- Hyper-startled response

- Compulsive behaviors

- Withdrawal and isolation

- Family discord

- Crying spells and disconnected stares

- Violence and antisocial behavior

**I. Physical Symptoms of Post-Traumatic Stress**

- Rapid or slowed heartbeat

- Headaches

- Hyperventilating or muscle spasms

- Psychogenic sweating

- Extreme fatigue or exhaustion

- Indigestion, nausea, vomiting

- Blood in stool, sputum, vomit, or urine

- Chest pain or loss of consciousness

J. **Spiritual Symptoms of Post-Traumatic Stress**

- Anger directed at God

- Withdrawal from faith-based community

- Clinging to faith

K. **Learning skills of assessment is key to effective crisis intervention.**

L. **Crisis interventionists need to help victims understand that the symptoms they are experiencing are a normal reaction to an abnormal event.**

## III. Cautions

A. **Beware of the principle of vicarious traumatization.**

- People can be traumatized by hearing about trauma that someone else experienced.

- Circles of Impact/Homogeneous Groups – people grouped together should all have been impacted similarly and all should be witnesses of the traumatic event.

B. **The crisis response provider will need to get care for himself/herself.**

## IV. Conclusion

A. **Anyone who has adequate training can provide crisis intervention.**

B. **Crisis intervention should be performed by teams.**

C. Churches should form crisis response teams, support groups, and training programs for helping those that have experienced crisis, trauma, or loss.

D. Crisis intervention is about immediate response, so responders must be prepared in advance.

E. Christians have the primary component of healing to offer to those who are hurting, and that component is hope.

## CCCT 201 Study Questions

1. Discuss the three dynamics of modern crisis intervention.

2. What are the purposes of psychological first aid?

3. Who should crisis responders consider for follow-up services?

4. Compare and contrast the general, emotional, behavioral, physical, and spiritual symptoms of post-traumatic stress.

5. Discuss the principle of vicarious traumatization, and how this practically applies to crisis response.

# CCCT 202
# METHODS AND TECHNIQUES FOR IMMEDIATE RESPONSE
## Thomas Webb, Th.M.

## Course Description

This lesson overviews the process of Critical Incident Stress Management (CISM) with a focus on spiritual crisis intervention. How does one bear another's burden when the victim expresses deep spiritual distress in the form of questions such as "Why did God allow my child to die?" or "I feel like God has abandoned me!" Chaplain Thomas Webb will guide students through assessment criteria for crisis intervention, particularly that of a spiritual nature.

## Learning Objectives

By the end of this lesson, students:

1.  Will be able to know the basic terms of crisis intervention, as well as the multiple types of CISM interventions.

2.  Will be able to know the identity and purpose of a spiritual crisis interventionist.

3.  Will be able to know the assessment criteria for spiritual crisis intervention.

## I. Definitions

A. The field of "crisis intervention" encompasses (1) providing material aid, such as food, shelter, clothing, aid in processing insurance and (2) providing crisis care to individuals overwhelmed from the traumatic stress of a critical incident.

B. The term "crisis" refers to the state of impairment in functioning that a person experiences first physically, cognitively, and emotionally and then later impairment in relationships horizontally with family and friends and vertically with God.

C. The term "critical incident" refers to any event that an individual experiences and results in a state of impairment in functioning physically, psychologically, and relationally.

D. An Overview Chart of Existing Crisis Intervention Models

| Critical Incident Stress Debriefing (Dr. Jeff Mitchell) | Psychological Debriefing (Dr. A. Dyregrov) | Group Crisis Intervention (National Organization for Victim Assistance) | Multiple-Stressor Debriefing (American Red Cross) | Critical Event Debriefing (Dr. J. Stokes) |
|---|---|---|---|---|
| 1 Introduction | Introduction | Introduction | Event | Introduction |
| 2. Fact | Fact | Event | Feelings and Reactions | Chronological Reconstruction |
| 3. Thought | Thought | Aftermath | Coping | Cognitive-Affective Reactions |
| 4. Reaction | Sensory | Expectations Future | Termination | Symptoms |
| 5. Symptoms | Normalization | Education | | Teaching (Coping Strategies) |
| 6. Teaching (Coping Strategies) | Closure | Conclusion | | Wrap-up |
| 7. Re-entry | Follow-up Debriefing | | | |

E. The common goal of each of these models is to help small groups of individuals to regain normal functioning (homeostasis or balance) physically, psychologically, and relationally.

F. The most effective means of conducting crisis intervention is using a multi-component response system that strategically assesses the impairment of individuals and employs the most suitable intervention to use at the appropriate time.

G. "In all the controversy, criticism and research debate on the merits of debriefing [early intervention], certain constants are emerging. *The most effective methods for mitigating the effects of exposure to trauma* ..., those which will help keep our people healthy and in service, *are those which use early intervention, are multi-modal and multi-component.* That is, they use different 'active ingredients' ... and these components are used at the appropriate time with the right target group." (Dr. Hayden Duggan)

## II. Critical Incident Stress Management (CISM) from the International Critical Incident Stress Foundation (ICISF)

A. The ICISF's model of CISM is recognized by the United Nations and by federal and state agencies.

B. CISM represents an approach to crisis intervention, which is:

- comprehensive (in scope of pre-, mid-, and post-crisis).

- phase sensitive (to changing states of individual's level of impairment and functioning).

- integrated (interventions complimentary in restoring functioning).

- multi-component (variety of interventions to address specific needs).

### C. Chart of ICISF Multi-Component Crisis Intervention Tactics

| Intervention | Timing | Target Group | Potential Goals |
|---|---|---|---|
| **Pre-incident Planning and Preparation** | Prior to critical incident occurring | Anticipated population groups | Anticipate guidance<br>Foster resistance to stress<br>Promote resilience |
| **Assessment** | Pre-intervention | Those directly and indirectly exposed | Determine need for intervention |
| **Strategic Planning** | Pre-event and during event | Anticipated exposed and victim populations | Critically plan crisis response |
| **Individual Crisis Intervention** | As needed | Individuals as identified | Assessment<br>Psychological and spiritual first aid<br>Education<br>Facilitate continued support |

| Intervention | Timing | Target Group | Potential Goals |
|---|---|---|---|
| **Large Group Crisis Intervention** | | | |
| A. Demobilization | At shift disengagement | Emergency personnel | Decompression<br>Ease transition<br>Triage<br>Facilitate follow-up |
| B. Respite Center | Ongoing at large scale incidents | Emergency personnel | Refreshment<br>Triage<br>Support |
| C. Crisis Management Brief | As needed | Heterogeneous large groups | Inform<br>Control rumors<br>Increase cohesion |
| **Small Group Crisis Intervention** | | | |
| D. Crisis Management Brief | As needed | Heterogeneous small groups seeking resources & information | Inform<br>Control rumors<br>Increase cohesion |
| E. Defusing | Ongoing events<br>Post-events within 12 hours | Small homogeneous groups (similar experience of trauma experience) | Stabilization<br>Reduce acute distress<br>Information<br>Facilitate resilience |
| F. Group Debriefing (CISD) | Post-Event<br>G. 1-10 days for acute events<br>H. 3-4 weeks post-disaster recovery phase | Small homogeneous groups (similar experience of trauma experience) | Assessment<br>Psychological and spiritual first aid<br>Education<br>Facilitate continued support |

| Intervention | Timing | Target Group | Potential Goals |
|---|---|---|---|
| **Family Crisis Intervention** | Pre-event<br>As needed during and post-event | Families | Pre-event preparation<br>Individual and small group interventions (CMB, Defusing, CISD) |
| **Organizational/ Community Intervention and Consultation** | Pre-event<br>As needed during and post-event | Organizations/ communities affected by critical incident | Improve organizational preparedness and response<br>Consult leadership |
| **Pastoral Crisis Intervention** | As needed | Individuals or groups who desire faith-based presence and crisis intervention | Faith-based support<br>Restore spiritual functioning in relationship with God |
| **Follow-up/ Referral** | As needed | Intervention recipients and exposed individuals | Assure continuity of care |

## III. Application of CISM in the Community

### A. Requirements for Forming a Church CISM Team

- Identifying the people whom the team will serve (church members and community)

- Establishing the business operating identity (a separate non-profit corporation or function as a ministry of the church)

- Recruiting and training team members (mental health professional and peers)

- Developing relationships with the identified population to be served

- Raising funding for the team's operation

### B. Benefits of a CISM Team

- Provides an effective and efficient means to show the love of God to neighbors in need of spiritual and emotional first aid, which otherwise might be neglected

- Builds relationship bonds that may open discussions about the Gospel

- Enables churches to have a cadre of trained crisis care-givers to attend to members' crisis needs (when hospitalized, after learning of a life-threatening illness, such as cancer, or sudden unemployment or loss of a home)

- Provides a recognized means to work with government officials at disaster sites

## IV. Assessing and Responding to a Spiritual Cry of Distress Versus a Crisis of Faith

A. **Assess first the nature and severity of the critical incident: "How big was the rock tossed into the pond?"**

- Type of critical incident (fire, flood, car accident, shooting, bombing, etc.)

- Severity (of injuries, of deaths, of nature of violence, of property loss)

- Primary shock wave victims (those closest to critical incident)

- Secondary shock wave victims (those impacted by ripples of shock wave)

- Duration of the event

B. **Assess the Impact on the Individual**

- By observing the following about impacted individuals:

   1) speech (rapid, slow, halting)

   2) emotion (fear, panic, anger, despair, shock)

   3) appearance (disheveled, tattered, bloody)

   4) activity level (hyper alert, hyper active, lethargic)

   5) alertness (concrete thoughts, tangential thoughts)

- By noting the symptoms in the following categories:

   1) physical (vacant stare, rapid heart and breathing rate, sweating)

   2) cognitive (trouble making decisions, difficulty with memory)

   3) emotional (fear, panic, anger, helplessness, hopelessness, despair)

   4) behavioral (withdrawal and/or difficulty in relationships, eating/sleeping changes)

   5) spiritual (anger at God, despair, loss of spirit of thankfulness, no desire to continue with righteous living)

### C. Assessing and Responding to a Spiritual Cry of Distress and a Crisis of Faith

| Assessment Criteria | Spiritual Cry of Distress | Crisis of Faith |
|---|---|---|
| **Time elapsed from the impact of the critical incident** | • Relatively soon | • Later (after some days of attempting to interact in relationships) |
| **Prevalent Trauma Symptoms** | • Physical shock conditions (vacant stare)<br>• Cognitive Impairment<br>• Emotional Distress | • Behavioral impairment in horizontal relationships with family, etc.<br>  o withdrawal (retreats from social interaction of family and workplace)<br>  o inability to communicate and gain support (arguments/ frustration/despair)<br>• Spiritual impairment in vertical relationships with God<br>  o lack of a spirit of thankfulness<br>  o God seems distant and one's normal theological worldview seems useless in making sense of life |
| **Relational Context** | • Focus on self and one's state of being | • Focus on impairment in relationships horizontally and vertically<br>• "No one seems to understand – not my wife, not my friends, not even God!" |
| **Crisis Intervention Goal** | • Restore from the state of shock to functioning in relationships horizontally and vertically | • Restore hope and a spirit of thankfulness in relationships |

### D. Responding in Spiritual Alignment to Individuals Overwhelmed with Traumatic Stress

- Hearing the cry of the individual requires hearing accurately their expression of spiritual and emotional distress and validating through a paraphrase.

- Exploring the significance of the relationship impacted by the critical incident further provides a sense of validation of the individual and bolsters hope as the ambassador of God has heard their cry.

**CCCT 202 Study Questions**

1. What are the purposes of crisis intervention?

2. In assessing a critical incident, what should one examine?

3. In assessing the impact on an individual, what should one examine?

4. Discuss the implications of spiritual crisis intervention, and when crisis responders should approach a situation using spiritual crisis intervention.

5. Define the terms "crisis intervention," "crisis," and "critical incident."

# CCCT 203
# PEER SUPPORT AND ACCOUNTABILITY
## Joshua Straub, Ph.D. Candidate

## Course Description

This lesson discusses the importance of peer support and accountability regarding crisis intervention. Joshua Straub will address key principles regarding crisis intervention as it relates to having a strong support system in place for the individuals who experience crises in their lives. He will also give students cautions regarding peer support, so that they will know how to properly intervene in a crisis context.

## Learning Objectives

By the end of this lesson, students:

1. Will be able to understand the role of the family and of the church in crisis intervention.

2. Will be able to learn what the SAFER model is, and how it should be used.

3. Will be able to understand what the Bible says about crisis intervention.

CCCT 203

# I. Effective interventions for Preventing PTSD

### A. Proximity

### B. Immediacy

### C. Expectancy

# II. Crisis Intervention

### A. The purpose of crisis intervention is to intervene effectively, as immediately as possible, as close to the event as possible, creating expectancy to heal.

### B. Crisis responders help victims of crisis put language to the event, allowing them to effectively talk about what they have been through.

### C. It is critically important to establish peer support and accountability.

### D. PTSD Prevalence

- 10-15% of law enforcement officers

- 10-30% of firefighters

- 16% of Vietnam veterans

- 20% of Iraq War veterans

# III. Peer Support

### A. Establishing Credibility

- Use a peer when recipient group member is specially educated or trained.

- Develop rapport and credibility among the group members.

- Use a peer when the group member extends minimal trust to outsiders.

- It is not typically necessary to use peers when working with a general population of victims.

### B. Cautions Regarding Peer Support

- Consider the need for a mental health professional.

- Understand that crisis intervention is psychological first aid.

- Know when one is over his/her head and make a referral.

- Be mindful of countertransference.

### C. Importance of Family and Family Intervention

- Educate the family about important factors and considerations.

- Teach stress management techniques.

- Teach family how to tell the story in a safe way.

- Recognize when to refer as a family.

### D. What Not to Do

- Do not argue about their experience or minimize their problem.

- Do not over-spiritualize their experience.

- Do not use Christian clichés.

## IV. The S.A.F.E.R. Model

### A. STABILIZE the situation.

### B. ACKNOWLEDGE the crisis.

C. FACILITATE the understanding that they are having a normal reaction to an abnormal event.

D. ENCOURAGE effective coping and mechanisms of action.

- Teach stress management.

- Information is key – crisis responders can't overeducate the symptoms they might experience.

- What helped them in the past?

- Frontal lobe not functioning correctly; don't make major life decisions.

- Help them resolve conflict.

- Don't discount the power of the Holy Spirit to transform and change lives, and to heal people.

E. RECOVERY and REFERRAL

## V. What the Bible Says Regarding Crisis Intervention

A. Psalm 19:14 – *"Let the words of my mouth and the meditation of my heart be acceptable in Your sight, O Lord, my rock and my redeemer."*

B. Acts 4:13 – *"Now when they saw the boldness of Peter and John, and perceived that they were uneducated, common men, they were astonished. And they recognized that they had been with Jesus."*

## CCCT 203 Study Questions

1. Discuss the effective interventions necessary for preventing PTSD.

2. What does it mean to establish peer support and accountability in a crisis context? What would this look like?

3. Discuss the importance of family and family intervention.

4. What are some of the cautions that were discussed regarding peer support?

5. Discuss each component of the S.A.F.E.R. model.

## CCCT 204
# SURVIVOR GUILT AND FOSTERING RESILIENCY
### Kevin Ellers, D.Min.

## Course Description

Following traumatic events, survivors frequently struggle with a broad range of thoughts, feelings, and reactions as they try to put their lives back together in the post-trauma journey. Feelings of guilt are common during this road to recovery. Dr. Kevin Ellers will discuss the critical role that the church can play through this process in helping to help people grow through the adverse circumstances by enhancing resiliency in the pre- and post-trauma journey.

## Learning Objectives

By the end of this lesson, students:

1. Will be able to define critical elements of survivor guilt, and identify ways to help people distinguish between true and false guilt while learning the purpose of guilt.

2. Will be able to effectively discuss specific interventions for survivor guilt, as well as define key elements of resiliency.

3. Will be able to identify biblical principles for coping with adversity, and discuss ways in which the church can foster and sustain resiliency and hope.

# I. Survivor Guilt Following Traumatic Events

**A. Typical definition** – wondering "why them and not me" after surviving a traumatic incident in which others lost their lives.

**B. Broader definition** – the "if only" statements that can color, or discolor, the rest of a person's life.

**C. Guilt has both affective and cognitive elements.** Guilt stems from internal beliefs, not by the external cause.

**D. Guilt may be viewed in two categories:**

- Real guilt – involves acts of omission or commission that endangered or contributed to harm of self and/or others

- Imagined guilt – wishful thinking about one's ability to have chosen a different course of action that would have in some way impacted the event and altered the outcome

**E. Shame is the close cousin of guilt.** Guilt says, "I did something wrong," and shame says, "I am a bad person for what I did."

**F. Four Functions of Guilt**

- Defends against helplessness

- Effects self-punishment

- Inhibits impulses

- Prevents the event from becoming meaningless

**G. Guilt Can Also**

- Stop people from doing something that is wrong

- Motivate people to make amends for intentionally or unintentionally hurting others

- Help people anticipate bad decisions before engaging in harmful behavior

- Mask other issues such as grief

- Defend people against powerlessness

## II. Helping Survivors Process Feelings of Guilt in the Aftermath of Trauma and Loss

A. Help by providing a safe environment for people to express their feelings of guilt.

B. Help by letting people understand their trauma story.

C. Help people understand how they feel guilt.

D. Explore the factors that contribute to feelings of guilt.

E. Romans 4 teaches that actions should be based upon internal convictions.

F. Shame is lethal.

G. Mourning the loss is an important step in healing.

H. Teach survivors the body's natural response to stress.

I. Help survivors understand the human survival response.

J. The body may shut down totally or time may seem to slow down.

K. True guilt comes from God. False guilt comes from Satan.

L. Help survivors see their survival as a gift from God.

M. Guilt can be adaptive when it serves to lead to transformative changes within one's character, perceptions, and actions.

## III. Fostering Resiliency in Trauma Survivors

### A. Churches have a powerful role in enhancing resiliency.

- Importance of painting a real picture of suffering and adversity in life.

- Nietzsche's famous statement, "That which does not kill me makes me stronger," rings true for many survivors.

- Many Scriptures confirm the adversity of life for most human beings and yet clearly portray that in this adversity, believers can grow and mature.

  1) Ecclesiastes 11:8

  2) 1 Peter 4:12-19

- God has promised to be with His people and that He understands their suffering.

  1) Isaiah 53:3-4

  2) Hebrews 4:14-16

### B. Resiliency is the Ability To:

- cope well with high levels of ongoing disruptive change.

- sustain good health and energy in the midst of stress.

- bounce back from setbacks.

- overcome adversity.

- change to new ways of working and living when an old way is impossible.

- accomplish all of this without acting dysfunctionally

C. **Personality Traits of Resilient People**

- Extroversion

- High self-esteem

- Assertiveness

- Hardiness

- Internal locus of control

- Cognitive level of feedback

D. **Ego-Resistance - Flexibility, energy assertiveness, humor, transcendent attachment, and a good capacity for affect regulation.**

E. **Resiliency is something people do, rather than something that they have.**

F. **The Latin root of resiliency means to "jump back."**

G. **Resiliency is multi-dimensional. People are both traumatized and resilient at the same time.**

H. **Help people understand that the experience of trauma will change.**

I. **Continental Divide Principle – "Stress can strengthen some people or break others altogether." – Abraham Maslow**

SURVIVOR GUILT AND FOSTERING RESILIENCY

**J. Post-traumatic resilience is associated with ego resilience which includes:**

- Flexibility

- Energy assertiveness

- Humor

- Transcendent detachment

- Good capacity for affect regulation

**K. How do people enhance resiliency?**

- The caregiver should explore core disruptions in the following areas to help survivors rebuild.

    1) safety

    2) trust

    3) control

    4) esteem intimacy

- Assessing vulnerability

    1) coping strategies and styles

    2) age or developmental level of the traumatized individual

    3) personal gender-specific characteristics

    4) social-cognitive factors

    5) the stress and symptoms experienced by close family members

- Assessing the survivor's view

  1) define the reality of the situation

  2) accept responsibility and avoid blame

  3) maintain good physical, emotional, and spiritual health

  4) develop good thinking and problem-solving skills

  5) establish healthy boundaries to keep good in and bad out

  6) mobilize toward positive, manageable actions steps

- Johns Hopkins Model – create resistance, enhance resiliency, and speed recovery

## IV. Conclusion

A. Romans 5:2-5 – *"Through Him we have also obtained access by faith into this grace in which we stand, and we rejoice in hope of the glory of God. Not only that, but we rejoice in our sufferings, knowing that suffering produces endurance, and endurance produces character, and character produces hope, and hope does not put us to shame, because God's love has been poured into our hearts through the Holy Spirit who has been given to us."*

B. "The beautiful people are those who have known defeat, known suffering, known struggle, known loss and have found their way out of the depths. These people have appreciation and sensitivity and an understanding of life that fills them with compassion, gentleness, and a deep, loving concern. Beautiful people do not just happen." – Elizabeth Kübler-Ross

## CCCT 204 Study Questions

1. Compare and contrast real guilt and imagined guilt.

2. Discuss the functions of guilt, and why it is important to understand guilt's role in a person's life

3. How can one help survivors process feelings of guilt in the aftermath of trauma and loss?

4. How can the church help foster resiliency in trauma survivors?

5. Discuss the importance of assessing both vulnerability and the survivor's view when processing guilt and fostering resiliency in trauma survivors.

# CCCT 205
# MANAGING THE HIGH COST OF CARE
## Eric Scalise, Ph.D.

## Course Description

In this lesson, Dr. Eric Scalise will discuss the importance of self-care and give resources and clear guidance regarding self-assessment. The world today is one full of stress and trauma, and those in the ministry or helping profession need to become educated on the topic of compassion fatigue. Dr. Scalise will discuss how caregivers can take care of themselves, develop a personal stress prevention care plan and survive counseling stress.

## Learning Objectives

By the end of this lesson, students:

1. Will be able to understand both the building blocks and consequences of stress, and learn how people handle expectations.

2. Will be able to understand the concept of compassion fatigue and why it is important to those in the helping profession.

3. Will be able to learn practical ways to self-assess and survive counseling stress.

## I. General Principles Regarding Stress

**A. This world is full of stress and trauma.**

**B. The church needs to be the people who help address this trauma and stress.**

**C. Culture today tends to define success in quantitative numbers, but people need to consider qualitative indicators.**

**D. Individual expectations might be legitimate, but the composite expectations may be overwhelming.**

**E. Counselors and ministry leaders are often not allowed to fail, hurt, or be human.**

**F. As stress increases, so does resistance to getting help, producing crises.**

**G. People must consider boundaries to be an important principle.**

**H. It is often the journey and the process of working through the pain, trauma, grief, and loss that brings survival, health, and growth.**

**I. How Expectations are Often Handled**

- Preoccupation with stress-producing situations or individuals

- Overindulgence in escape behaviors

- Avoidance of intimacy in favor of fantasy

- Controlling the environment

- Leaving the profession or ministry

### J. Building Blocks of Stress

- Role Ambiguity – "What am I supposed to be doing?"

- Role Conflict – "Am I doing the right thing?"

- Role Overload – "Am I doing too much?"

- Role Inconsequentiality – "Is what I'm doing really making a difference?"

- Role Isolation – "Am I alone too much?"

- Role Rigidity – "Am I still in control?"

### K. Consequences of Stress

- Stress is "the nonspecific response of the body on any demand." – Dr. Hans Selye

- Can have a psychosocial or biogenic orientation

- Adrenaline and cortisol

  1) Constricts capillaries

  2) Reduces the body's ability to flush out bad cholesterol

  3) Promotes heart disease

  4) Impacts a person's ability for short-term memory and can cause cognition problems

- 25% of all prescriptions written are for psychotropic drugs. – U.S. Dept. of Health and Human Services

## II. Compassion Fatigue

### A. The term was first coined in the early 1990s by Charles Figley.

### B. It is sometimes referred to as secondary or vicarious trauma.

C. **The effects of stress, such as sleep loss, are cumulative.**

D. **Two Types of Stress**

- The stress of the ministry or profession

- The stress brought into the ministry or profession

- "Is my profession causing the stress and problems in my life, or is it revealing the stress and problems in my life?"

E. **Surviving Counseling Stress**

- Learn to depersonalize the process and limit time around negative people.

- Don't forget one's First Love because a person is not the ministry.

- Learn to rest and slow down the pace of change.

- Learn to be silent and still.

- Seek to give one's burdens to God every day.

- Learn to triage one's daily and life events.

- Learn to have realistic expectations of oneself and others.

- Laugh. Do not lose the capacity for joy.

- Pay attention to one's diet and exercise.

- Learn to resolve those things that can be attended to quickly and easily.

- Learn to manage one's time by saying "no."

- Learn to delegate.

- Find one or two key people in one's life to be accountable to.

## III. Conclusion

A. John 16:33 – *"I have said these things to you, that in Me you may have peace. In the world you will have tribulation. But take heart; I have overcome the world."*

B. What is God impressing on one's life to change?

## CCCT 205 Study Questions

1. What were some of the ways mentioned in the video that people tend to handle expectations? Are these ways healthy?

2. Discuss the building blocks of stress.

3. How are adrenaline and cortisol linked to stress, and why is this important to understand?

4. What is compassion fatigue?

5. What are some areas that one needs to personally change that would foster better self-care and help one survive the stress of counseling?

# CCCT 206
# COMMUNITY RESPONSE AND CULTURAL DIFFERENCES
## Leroy Scott, M.S., M.Div. & Pat Miersma, Ph.D.

### Course Description

Cultural competence is an important element of working with individuals that have experienced trauma or crisis situations. Community responses and cultural differences impact the effectiveness of service delivery. The presenters will address issues such as how to engage a client from a different culture, the importance of community and involvement in urban communities, and how to get through the red tape, politics, and protocol to provide the highest quality service possible. This lesson defines the basic components of cultural competence in treating victims of crisis and trauma.

### Learning Objectives

By the end of this lesson, students:

1. Will be able to develop an understanding of the need for cultural sensitivity in crisis and trauma responses.

2. Will be able to identify strategies for addressing issues concerning community based resources, politics, and red tape.

3. Will be able to review the impact of multicultural differences within families in providing crisis intervention.

## I. Why Be Culturally Sensitive?

A. God cares for humanity, which encompasses a variety of people, ethnicities, and cultures.

B. Culture impacts a person's thoughts, understanding, relevance of suffering, and expression of feelings.

C. Language influences both expression, as well as options, for obtaining help.

## II. Cultural Competency

A. A primary focus of cultural competency should be joining and connecting with a family member to empower that family toward the truth.

B. When the helper really begins to understand the culture of another person, there is an opportunity to differentiate themselves, as well as an opportunity to avoid prejudices.

C. The culturally competent helper spends a vast amount of time learning about the culture they seek to help.

D. Do not take for granted that a common American response to a crisis will be the same for a person from a different culture.

E. Domestic crisis response occurs at three levels: federal, state, and local.

F. The more impoverished, disenfranchised, and economically broken the community, the fewer resources are available.

G. The church has a significant responsibility in reaching out to the community.

## III. Trauma and Culture

A. When people experience trauma, they seek to find meaning and a way to express that meaning.

B. Not only is the body affected in a trauma; the mind, the soul, and the spirit are impacted as well.

C. The Word of God can break through and transcend cultures, not only by valuing and affirming culture, but also by bringing light to show how things in culture can lead people astray.

D. The first 72 hours are critical and the main thing people need to know is that someone is there to help.

E. In a crisis of faith, a counselor can be there until a person is ready to deal with their questions.

## CCCT 206 Study Questions

1. Discuss various reasons regarding why it is important to be culturally sensitive as someone in the helping profession.

2. Specifically, what does culture impact about a person?

3. The presenters discussed the role of the church, and how it has a significant responsibility in helping people of all different cultures in trauma situations. What could this practically look like in a person's local city?

4. Discuss the following statement referenced in the video: "The Word of God can break through and transcend cultures ..."

5. What are some ways that one can personally enhance his/her cultural competency?

# UNIT THREE
# POST-TRAUMATIC STRESS DISORDER

# CCCT 301
# SIGNS AND SYMPTOMS OF PTSD
Michael Lyles, M.D.

## Course Description

In this lesson, students will become familiar with a general overview of Post-Traumatic Stress Disorder (PTSD). Dr. Michael Lyles will discuss the signs and symptoms of PTSD, the nature of trauma, and the diagnostic criteria regarding this disorder. Students will also gain an understanding of the challenges that helpers and counselors can face in trauma sufferers. Because people dealing with symptoms of PTSD are literally reliving their traumatic experiences, it is important for students to understand important factors such as avoidance behavior, numbing effects, hyperarousal, and neurobiological issues.

## Learning Objectives

By the end of this lesson, students:

1. Will be able to understand the diagnostic criteria of PTSD.

2. Will be able to understand diagnostic difficulties, and learn questions for initiating dialogue regarding traumatic events.

3. Will be able to learn an overview of the neurobiological factors taking place in a person's brain while experiencing PTSD symptoms.

## I. Post-Traumatic Stress Disorder General Overview

**A. Definition** – An anxiety disorder that occurs after exposure to a traumatic event which triggers memories of the traumatic event and is characterized by intense fear, helplessness, and horror.

**B. Approximately 25-30% of victims of significant trauma develop PTSD.**

**C. Trauma**

- Trauma can occur from witnessing or experiencing a traumatic event.

- Trauma can occur from trying to help someone deal with a traumatic event.

- The risk for PTSD varies with severity, duration, and subjective experience of the trauma.

- Traumatic Events

    1) natural disasters

    2) automobile accidents

    3) rape or sexual molestation

    4) airplane crash

    5) torture

    6) physical assault

    7) terrorist attack

    8) witnessing the death of another person

### D. Symptoms

- usually begin within three months of the trauma (can begin years later)

- occurs for longer than a month

- keeps a person from living a normal life

## II. Diagnosing PTSD

### A. Diagnostic Criteria

- Exposure to a traumatic event with both of the following:

  1) The person experienced, witnessed, or was confronted with an event(s) that involved actual or threatened death or serious injury, or a threat to the physical integrity of self or others.

  2) The person's response involved intense fear, helplessness, or horror.

- Repeatedly thinking about the trauma. Trauma is persistently relived in at least one of the following:

  1) recurrent, upsetting, intrusive memories

  2) recurrent, upsetting dreams

  3) acting/feeling as if the event was occurring now

  4) intense psychological or physiological distress with exposure to internal or external triggers of the event

- Avoiding reminders of the trauma (can be avoiding triggers of the trauma or numbing one's feelings so one does not experience reminders). Must be indicated by three (or more) of the following categories:

  1) efforts to avoid thoughts, feelings, or conversations

  2) numbing of general responsiveness that was not present before the trauma

  3) avoidance of activities, places, or people

  4) inability to recall an important aspect of the trauma

5) marked decrease of interest or participation in pleasurable activities

6) feeling detached or estranged from others

7) feeling restricted range of emotions

8) sense of doom that something bad is just going to happen; it's just a matter of time

9) assuming the worst

- Being constantly alert or on guard. Must have two or more of the following persistent symptoms of increased arousal (not present before the trauma):

    1) difficulty falling or staying asleep

    2) irritability or anger outbursts

    3) difficulty concentrating

    4) hypervigilance

    5) exaggerated startle response

## B. Making the Diagnosis

- Symptoms last for more than a month, and not present prior to the trauma

- Symptoms cause clinically significant distress or impairment in social, occupational, or other important areas of functioning

- Acute Stress Disorder (resolves within a month)

- Acute PTSD (lasts less than three months)

- Chronic PTSD (lasts three months or more)

- Delayed Onset (begins six or more months after the traumatic event)

### C. Diagnostic Difficulties

- Patient does not link symptoms with trauma

- Patient does not want to talk about the traumatic event

- Other symptoms/problems demand more attention

- Patient focuses on physical symptoms

### D. Questions for Initiating Dialogue

- "Were there missions on which you encountered life threatening situations?"

- "Were you ever in a situation where you feared for your life?"

- "Were you in situations where team members were wounded?"

- "Did you ever participate in any situations that involved the loss of life – friend or enemy?"

- "Did you unexpectedly witness a dead body or dead body parts?"

## III. PTSD Challenges

### A. Common Challenges

- Guilt, shame

- Self-destructive, impulsive behaviors

- Feeling permanently damaged

- Feeling constantly threatened

- Feeling ineffective

- Despair, hopelessness

- Hostility, personality change

- Loss of previously sustained beliefs

- Social withdrawal, impaired relationships

- Dissociative symptoms

- Somatic symptoms

**B. Especially Difficult Challenges**

- Self-medicating behaviors

- Depression and suicidal thoughts

- Panic attacks, feelings of mistrust

**C. Co-Existing Conditions**

- A National Co-Morbidity Survey found that 88.3% of men and 79% of women with PTSD have at least one other psychiatric problem (usually depression).

- 59% of men and 44% of women meet criteria for three or more psychiatric disorders.

- Co-Existing Disorders

  1) Depression

  2) Alcohol/Substance Abuse Disorders

  3) Phobias

  4) Social Anxiety Disorder

  5) Panic Disorder

  6) Eating Disorder

  7) Obsessive-Compulsive Disorder

## IV. Course of PTSD

    A. Duration of symptoms is affected by the intensity, duration, subjective interpretation, and proximity of the trauma.

    B. Symptoms may come and go.

    C. Average duration for treated patients: 36 months

    D. Average duration for untreated patients: 64 months

    E. More than one-third never recover.

    F. About 50% recover within the first three months.

    G. PTSD symptoms only occur in a minority of patients exposed to trauma, so something must be different with those who develop PTSD.

## V. Biology of the Brain in People Who Develop PTSD

    A. The Emotional Brain (Limbic System)

    B. Amygdala – activated by the sympathetic nervous system when danger is present. The "HOT" system.

    C. Hippocampus – filters the threat through emotional memory filters to evaluate the nature of the threat. The "COOL" system.

    D. Cingulate – the decision-maker regarding impulse control and course of action.

### E. Brain Imaging Studies

- Small hippocampus (COOL System)

- Hyperactive amygdala (HOT System)

- Inactive cingulated cortex (No mediator)

- The result: All accelerator and no brakes or steering.

### F. The HPA System Chain of Command

- The cortisol engages the stressful threat and "handles" it with the appropriate intervention.

- The high cortisol levels feedback to the HPA system to turn the speed of cortisol production down – like cruise control on a car – to keep cortisol levels from peaking too high for too long (not healthy for heart, pancreas, lipids, etc.)

### G. The System is Different in PTSD

| Normally | With PTSD |
|---|---|
| Cortisol increases with stress | Cortisol decreases with stress |
| Few cortisol receptors (radar) in pituitary & hypothalamus because the cortisol signal is so strong | More radar (cortisol receptors) because the cortisol signal is so low |
| Feedback inhibition works properly (cruise control) | Feedback inhibition is "trigger happy" and over-responds to cortisol changes (cruise control overreacts to manual pedal and speeds up too fast) |

### H. The Chicken vs. Egg Debate. Are the physiological and anatomical changes the result of the trauma or were these changes present prior to the trauma, predisposing the person for PTSD?

## VI. Treatment

### A. When to Seek Help

- Symptoms for more than a month

- Affecting work, relationships, "peace of mind"

- Self-medicating with alcohol, drugs, etc.

- Progressively worsening symptoms

- Suicidal thoughts

**B. Good Prognostic Variables**

- Early intervention

- Early and ongoing social support

- Avoidance of re-traumatization

- Healthy lifestyle prior to the trauma

- Absence of psychiatric, substance abuse problems prior to the trauma

**C. Methods of Treatment**

- Psychotherapy

- Marital, family therapy

- Support groups

- Self-care

# VII. Conclusion

**A. What is learned in combat is never, ever forgotten.**

**B. Help providers cannot forget the pain and shame of the PTSD that hides behind the other problems in the lives of men and women long after the war is over.**

## CCCT 301 Study Questions

1. Give some examples of traumatic events that people experience. How could these differing events contribute to PTSD?

2. Briefly discuss the PTSD diagnostic criteria. Why is it important to know this information well?

3. Name some diagnostic difficulties that therapists could encounter with clients suffering from PTSD.

4. What are some co-existing conditions that some might have along with PTSD, and why are these important to recognize in a diagnosis?

5. When should someone seek help with symptoms of PTSD?

# CCCT 302
# RISK FACTORS FOR PTSD
Jennifer Cisney, M.A. & Chris Adsit, B.S.

## Course Description

There are many different kinds of trauma on the combat trauma spectrum that people can experience, and some can even be more predisposed than others for PTSD if they have certain risk factors. Jennifer Cisney will discuss what groups and individuals are more at risk for developing PTSD, what increases the risks, and what can be done on a preventative level for people who do fall into the high-risk categories.

## Learning Objectives

By the end of this lesson, students:

1.  Will be able to identify what groups and individuals fall into higher risk categories for developing PTSD.

2.  Will be able to understand what increases the risk within different high risk categories.

3.  Will be able to understand resiliency and what people can do on a preventative level.

## I. Risk Factors for PTSD

A. According to the Surgeon General's Report on Mental Illness, 9% of people exposed to traumatic events will develop PTSD (13% for females, 6% for males).

B. Collective Trauma – a blow to the basic tissues of social life that damages the bonds attaching people together and impairs the prevailing sense of community.

C. Who is at increased risk of developing PTSD?

- People who, due to their professions, are exposed at higher rates to a risk for PTSD

    1) What professions?

        (a) law enforcement personnel – 10-15%

        (b) firefighters – 10-30%

        (c) Vietnam veterans – 16%

        (d) Iraq & Afghanistan veterans – 12-20%

    2) What increases their risk?

        (a) close proximity to traumatic events

        (b) severity of traumatic events

        (c) duration of exposure

        (d) frequent or repeated exposure

- People who are exposed to a natural disaster or terrorist attack

    1) What increases their risk?

        (a) trauma collectively affects an entire community

        (b) physical devastation (injury or death)

      (c) social devastation

      (d) financial devastation

2) Phases of disaster impact

      (a) pre-disaster phase

      (b) heroic phase

      (c) honeymoon phase

      (d) disillusionment phase (most severe problems)

3) Terrorist attacks are different.

      (a) There was an intentional attack.

      (b) There is long-term affective anger.

4) With both natural disasters and terrorist attacks, there is a threat of trauma reoccurrence.

- Victims of violence and crime

1) 40-70% of rape victims will develop PTSD.

2) Rape victims carry a sense of stigma that is both internal and external.

3) School or workplace violence occurs in a place that carries an expectation of safety.

4) Victims of school or workplace violence have to return to the place where the trauma occurred.

5) Often the perpetrator of school or workplace violence is a person with whom the victims had a relationship.

- People with pre-existing conditions

  1) What increases their risk?

     (a) A high percentage of adults in today's society experienced childhood violence, abuse, or neglect.

     (b) Those with mental illness (anxiety or depression) are more apt to be triggered into PTSD due to their predisposition toward comorbid depression or anxiety.

     (c) Those with personality disorders which undermine a person's sense of self-efficacy, self-esteem, or self-worth which interfere with emotional self-regulation.

     (d) Those who have recent or a series of exposures to traumatic events when there has not been sufficient time to return to normal.

## II. Resiliency and Prevention

**A. Preventative Medicine. Encourage lifestyle changes NOW to reduce daily life stress and invest time in relationships with God, family, and fellow believers.**

**B. Factors that Improve Trauma Resiliency**

- Self-disclosure of the trauma to significant others

- A sense of group identity and a sense of self as a positive survivor

- Altruistic and pro-social behavior

- Capacity to find meaning in the trauma

- Connection with a significant community of friends and fellow survivors

## CCCT 302 Study Questions

1. Explain the concept of collective trauma.

2. Discuss the statistics regarding specific professions that expose people to having higher risks for PTSD. What increases their risk?

3. What increases the risk of developing PTSD in people who are exposed to a natural disaster or terrorist attack?

4. In victims of violence and crime, what increases the risk for developing PTSD?

5. What factors can increase a person's risk for developing PTSD when the person has pre-existing conditions?

# CCCT 303
# TRAUMA AND ADDICTION
## Mark Laaser, M.Div., Ph.D.

## Course Description

In this lesson, Dr. Mark Laaser will discuss the role of addiction regarding trauma. Students will learn about self-medicating tendencies and behaviors that people use to escape and numb the pain, the addictive cycle, factors related to tolerance, stages of addiction, and spiritual strongholds and bondage. After addressing the neurochemistry of addictions, Dr. Laaser will offer treatment approaches to ministering to people battling with addiction.

## Learning Objectives

By the end of this lesson, students:

1. Will be able to learn about trauma reactions, and how they are important in understanding addiction.

2. Will be able to understand the criteria for addiction, the addiction cycle, and addiction interaction regarding the neurochemical aspects of addiction.

3. Will be able to discuss treatment and healing processes of an addict, and discover that there is hope.

## I. Trauma Reactions

A. **Trauma Splitting (Dissociation)** – an ability to literally leave the body and be mentally and spiritually distant, absent, or gone

B. **Trauma Pleasure** – an adrenaline rush experienced during a wounding event

C. **Trauma Blocking** – any behavior or substance used to medicate the pain of woundedness

D. **Trauma Reactions** – the way the mind and body tells one there is woundedness inside

E. **Trauma Abstinence** – doing whatever is necessary to avoid the pain experienced in the past

F. **Trauma Shame** – the feeling that because of trauma one is a bad and worthless person

G. **Trauma Repetition** – the feeling that familiar behavior is safer than new behavior

H. **Trauma Bonding** – picking a relationship with another person that will help a person trauma repeat

## II. Addiction

A. Criteria

- Unmanageable

- Creates neurochemical tolerance

- Degenerative/progressive

- Creates destructive/negative consequences

B. **The Addiction Cycle**

- Preoccupation fantasy

- Ritual

- Acting out

- Despair

C. **Addiction Interaction**

D. **Stopping an addiction is only the beginning of the healing journey.**

# III. Healing

A. **Five Dimensions of Recovery**

- Spiritual

- Relational

- Personal

- Behavioral

- Physical

B. **Prefrontal Cortex Functions**

- Attention span

- Judgment

- Impulse control

- Organization

- Forward thinking

- Internal supervision

C. **Prefrontal Cortex Problems**

- Short attention span

- Impulsivity

- Procrastination

- Disorganization

- Poor judgment

- Lack of empathy and insight

D. **People must be assessed from a comorbid or dual diagnosis perspective.**

E. **Post-Traumatic Stress Disorder Diamond Pattern**

- Increased anterior cingulate

- Increased basal ganglia

- Increased thalamus (limbic)

- Increased right lateral temporal lobe

F. **Accountability**

- Involves a group

- Is proactive, not reactive

- Replaces unhealthy behaviors with healthy ones

G. **Intimacy problems in a marriage are not the result of addiction. The addiction is a coping mechanism for the intimacy difficulties.**

H. **Married addicts need threefold recovery: addict, spouse, and marriage recovery.**

I. **2 Corinthians 10:4** – *"For the weapons of our warfare are not of the flesh but have divine power to destroy strongholds."*

J. **2 Corinthians 10:5** – *"We destroy arguments and every lofty opinion raised against the knowledge of God, and take every thought captive to obey Christ."*

K. **Spiritual Dimension**

- Willingness

- Explore emotional and spiritual thirst

- Selflessness vs. selfishness

- Forgiveness

- Vision

## CCCT 303 Study Questions

1. Discuss each of the different trauma reactions, and why understanding these is essential in assessment.

2. What are the four stages of the addiction cycle?

3. What are the five dimensions of recovery, and which one is central to the others?

4. Explain the role of the prefrontal cortex in a traumatized person. What about in an addict?

5. Discuss the spiritual dimension of recovery. What should one examine within this dimension?

# CCCT 304
# SUICIDE ASSESSMENT AND PREVENTION
### Kevin Ellers, D.Min.

## Course Description

This lesson discusses the important topic of suicide assessment and prevention. Dr. Kevin Ellers addresses the issues of suicide being a by-product of traumatic events, risk factors related to suicide attempts, precipitating factors that would influence a person attempting suicide, warning signs, and effective intervention techniques. Students will begin to understand the dynamics of suicide and what caregivers can do to help.

## Learning Objectives

By the end of this lesson, students:

1. Will be able to dispel suicide myths and identify risk factors of suicide.

2. Will be able to understand motivations for suicide, and identify some life events that can trigger suicide.

3. Will be able to recognize signs of a suicide crisis and how to effectively provide intervention.

# I. Suicide

A. **Definition** – A conscious act of self-induced annihilation, best understood as a multidimensional malaise in a needful individual who defines an issue for which the act is perceived as the best solution.

B. **Survivor Reactions Following Suicide**

- Focus in early months on controlling the impact of the death

- Overwhelming need to make sense of the death

- Marked social uneasiness and stigma

- Eventual realization of purposefulness in life following the suicide death

C. **There is no evidence of total condemnation found in biblical accounts of suicide.**

D. **Most of the sense of condemnation people experience is societal.**

E. **Dispelling Myths About Suicide**

- Many times, a suicidal person has made up his/her mind and come to terms with the decision, resulting in an improvement in his/her mood prior to committing the act.

- It is not true that a person who has been suicidal at one time in life will always be suicidal.

- It is not true that people who are suicidal always intend to actually die; it is sometimes a cry for help.

- It is not true that suicide is hereditary.

- It is not true that if there is no note, there is no suicide.

F. **Risk Factors**

- Gender

    1) Males are four times more likely to complete suicide.

    2) Females are twice as likely to attempt without completing suicide.

- Age

    1) 85 years of age or older

    2) 75-84 years of age

- Depression or mental illness

    1) 30% of depression inpatients have attempted suicide.

    2) 90% of people who commit suicide have diagnosable mental illness.

    3) change in neurotransmitters or brain chemistry

- Previous exposure to suicide

    1) past history of attempting suicide

    2) genetic predisposition

- Substance abuse

- Irrational thinking/impulsivity

- Compromised social support network

- Emotional loss

- Marginalized individuals (loners)

## G. Motivations

- Loss or change in an important relationship

- Avoid or end perceived pain

- Escape an intolerable situation

- Gain attention

- Manipulate or punish others

- Become a martyr

## H. Life Events that Can Trigger Suicide

- Suicide of a loved one

- Death of a loved one

- Diagnosis of a serious illness

- Loss of health

- Divorce or separation

- Divorce and/or remarriage of parents

- Loss of employment

- Loss of cherished possessions

- Retirement

- Financial difficulties

- Legal problems/arrest

- Victims of crime, sexual abuse, or assault

- Witness of violence

- Poor grades

- College rejection

- Sexuality concerns

- Physical abuse

- Substance abuse

## II. Suicide Crisis

**A. A suicide crisis is a time limited occurrence that signals immediate danger that suicide may be imminent.**

**B. Signs of a Suicide Crisis**

- A precipitating event

- Intense affective states

- Changes in behavior

**C. Warning Signs of Suicide**

- Unrelenting low mood

- Sleep problems

- Making a plan

- Giving away prized possessions

**D. The emotional crisis that usually precedes a suicide is often recognizable and treatable.**

E. **Continuum of Suicidal Behavior**

- Ideation

- Gesture

- Attempt

- Completion

F. **Major Predictors of Suicidal Behavior**

- Is their plan specific?

- Availability of means

- Lethality of method

- Previous attempts

- What resources are available?

## III. Intervention

### A. Specific Questions to Ask

- "Have you been thinking of hurting or killing yourself?"

- "When did you last think seriously about completing suicide?"

- "Do you have the means available? Have you ever attempted suicide?"

- "Has anyone in your family ever completed suicide?"

- "What are the odds that you will leave and kill yourself?"

- "What has been keeping you alive so far?"

- "What do you think the future holds for you?"

## B. Effective Intervention – What to Do

- Do not panic or overreact. Remain calm.

- Remain with them. Be present and respect their feelings and thoughts.

- Help them reframe their thoughts.

- Emphasize the temporary nature of their problem.

- Keep yourself safe. Suicidal people are not rational.

- Explore alternatives and resources.

## C. Effective Intervention – What Not to Do

- Do not get into a lecturing or arguing situation.

- Do not overlook the signs.

- Do not express a sense of shock.

- Do not offer empty promises.

- Do not be overly cheery.

- Do not debate morality.

- Do not leave them alone or assume they will get better.

- Do not remain the ONLY person helping.

## CCCT 304 Study Questions

1. Discuss the myths of suicide that Dr. Ellers mentioned in the lesson.

2. What are some of the risk factors of suicide that caregivers should be aware of?

3. Give examples of life events that can trigger suicide.

4. What are some of the warnings of a suicide crisis?

5. Discuss the elements of effective intervention. What should one do and what should one not do?

# CCCT 305
# TREATMENT PROTOCOLS
## David Jenkins, Psy.D. & Michael Lyles, M.D.

## Course Description

This lesson will expose students to the wide range of treatment options in terms of theory and practice, including cognitive behavioral approaches to treatment, exposure theories, systematic desensitization methods, EMDR, medical protocol, and other related factors. Students will be exposed to a broad stroke at everything that needs to be considered when treating a person dealing with the difficult effects of PTSD as a process in helping someone move from absolute brokenness to abundant freedom.

## Learning Objectives

By the end of this lesson, students:

1. Will be able to understand three basic structures of the brain involved with people who are dealing with PTSD, and examine three symptom clusters that will explain what they may be experiencing.

2. Will be able to understand three basic treatment principles, regardless of the mode of counseling/therapy involved, that must be considered when treating people dealing with PTSD.

3. Will be able to understand the three broad treatment domains of exposure, cognitive-behavioral, and medical domains.

## I. Three Basic Structures

A. Amygdala – an organ in the brain that deals primarily with processing intense fear

B. Hippocampus – a part of the brain that is involved with memory processing

C. The HPA Axis – a hormonal type of system that is involved in the maintenance of stress response

D. Fear, memory, and meaning are locked into a pattern together and are responsible for thinking, concentration, judgment, smell, hearing, etc.

E. The amygdala and hippocampus are tied directly to emotional and thought systems in the brain – related to the many specific triggers for PTSD.

## II. Three Symptom Clusters

A. Re-Experiencing – can come in the form of recollections, dreams, nightmares, flashbacks, and physical/psychological reactivity

B. Avoidance/Numbing – can come in the form of avoiding situations, places, and/or people that remind the person of the traumatic event in order to manage response, detachment/feeling estranged, blanking out, and not being able to recall important aspects of the event

C. Hyperarousal/Hypervigilance – can come in the form of sleep difficulty, irritability, angry outbursts, difficulty with concentration, always being on the lookout, and exaggerated startle response

D. If someone is being affected by these symptom clusters, it is very important to have family or social support and involvement.

## III. Three Basic Treatment Principles

A. Address symptoms and co-morbid conditions. (Co-morbid conditions are other conditions that go along with PTSD; common ones are major depression, substance abuse, and specific anxiety disorders.)

B. Improve adaptive functioning and return the client to a state of safety and trust.

C. Limit generalization of initial trauma and protect against relapse.

## IV. Three Broad Treatment Domains

A. Exposure – a domain that involves facilitating the confrontation of feared objects, situations, images, and things that are associated with the traumatic event

- Exposure works by having the person purposefully interact with things that are troubling to him/her long enough that the fear response and the startle response in the symptom clusters arise in a protected, secure, and safe environment. The person needs to stay active long enough in that situation so that a different response can start to happen.

- Exposure can be imaginative, because PTSD events can be so vivid and brought that people can actually block out regular visual processing.

- Exposure can also be invivo (live), requiring the counselor to have the person go through the actual situation or experience in a place that evokes the PTSD symptoms. The client remains exposed to stimuli for a response to activate and then is altered in the direction of recovery.

- Exposure methods can be repeated over time in a series of interventions or in a prolonged fashion, where there is a lengthy session or repeated sessions over a longer period of time. The key is that the counselor does not want to activate a response and then shut it down too soon, whether he/she goes the repeated route or the prolonged exposure route. The counselor wants to prevent the person from escaping the painful feelings until they are processed in the session, or the counselor runs the risk of reinforcing the avoidance/numbing symptom cluster.

- Exposure can be particularly effective with intrusive symptoms.

- An example of an exposure method is systematic desensitization, which occurs in a graded way, where the counselor helps a person process through a hierarchy of anxious symptoms with the goal of helping replace an anxious response with a more relaxed, restful response.

- Another example is intensive exposure, which is non-graded. If a counselor chooses to use flooding, the person would be placed in a situation and then locked down – the person would stay there until the response settles down and then could be processed. If the counselor uses implosion, which is similar to flooding, the counselor would also fold in longer-term content, meanings, and symbolic types of interpretations to some of those symptoms.

B. **Cognitive-Behavioral Strategies – a domain that involves working with the modification of maladaptive thoughts, beliefs, and assumptions**

- There are key cognitions that tend to result from a tragic event. Some distorted assumptions are that protection from risk or harm is not under control, that the world is only dangerous and unpredictable, and that the person is inadequate and incapable.

- The results from the violation of key assumptions are the belief in personal invulnerability, the perception of the world as meaningful and predictable, and a positive view of self. These become violated and lead to those negative cognitions.

- The purpose of cognitive-behavioral strategies is to line up these cognitions with the truth and a respectful, honest view of self and others. People often take too much responsibility for a situation, such as a disaster like Hurricane Katrina, and a great amount of focus is going into a scenario that is not productive that they are not correctly managing the things that actually are under their control.

- Part of treatment involves lining up thoughts, behaviors, and feelings with reality-based living. This process helps restore a sense of dignity and responsibility within the person. This can also help place them on a path towards recovery; people begin to realize that they must still deal with the situation but that they are actually capable of dealing with it.

- A hallmark indicator of trauma is the shattering of a person's worldview. A necessary part of treatment involves restoring truth-based beliefs about God, the self, and the world, and those are the key components of helping restore the shattered worldview.

- One of the problems with cognitive-behavioral techniques is that if counselors fail to address the avoidance/numbing issues, then the clients will tend to avoid the very situations that can be helpful for them to confront so that they can challenge and restore some sense of normalcy. If people are dissociative/ numbing out/detaching relationships, that poses a challenge when working with someone using this kind of therapy.

- One specific technique that can be utilized is Eye Movement Desensitization Reprocessing (EMDR).

- EMDR is an information processing type of model that addresses how traumatic events tend to bypass normal memory and how it consolidates.

- EMDR helps activate memories that were encoded through the limbic system first. This is similar to the memory-forming process working backwards.

- EMDR involves accessing, processing, and resolving traumatic memories through desensitization of emotional stress, reformulation of associations and beliefs, and relief of physiological arousal.

- EMDR involves visualizing the worst moments of trauma while holding in mind current negative cognition, emotions, and sensations concerning the traumatic event.

- The client is attending to a concurrent stimulus while these negative cognitions are kept in mind. The counselor is tracking finger movements; the eyes moving are serving as a type of distraction while visualizing the worst moments, allowing the memories to be processed. This allows distance from traumatic images, allowing new thoughts and images to come to mind.

- EMDR involves reporting new images through oral or written communication.

- EMDR seems to overlap with exposure domains.

C. **Medical – Research shows that there are medications that can help with the treatment of PTSD. These medicines help to re-normalize brain function. However, many people will resist medication, while not recognizing that they are already self-medicating with means that are almost certainly more damaging than prescribed medical interventions.**

- Antidepressants

    1) enhance serotonin levels in the brain. (Serotonin is a hormone in the brain that occurs normally, and antidepressants help the brain have higher serotonin levels, or normal serotonin levels, depending on the patient.)

2) have the best track record in treating patients with PTSD symptoms

3) help reduce the stressful experience

4) The main side effects are the potential to gain weight, a possible decrease in libido, and the potential for upset stomach if taken without food.

5) non-addictive, non-habit forming, but must be tapered if coming off

- Adrenaline blockers

    1) block alpha and beta adrenaline blockers in the body and brain, but particularly in the body

    2) Adrenaline cannot work unless it has a place to attach on nerve and muscle cells.

    3) Adrenaline blockers work to block the receptors so that adrenaline does not have such an effect on the body, such as a high blood pressure or high pulse.

- Mood stabilizers

    1) can help the dramatic mood swings that a person can get with PTSD

    2) Someone with PTSD could experience mood swings with little provocation, and these drugs force people to go through the gradual pace of a normal mood swing.

    3) Examples of mood stabilizers are anticonvulsants and tranquilizers, and none of these drugs are addictive.

- Anti-anxiety medications

    1) These drugs can help with anxiety, but they are also addictive and can have withdrawal symptoms.

    2) There is also an added risk of overdose if someone drinks alcohol on top of taking these medications.

## V. Other Approaches

### A. Dual Representation Theory

- This theory addresses how memories are formed, stored, and accessed, and examines the effects of different types of memories and the effects they have as they work themselves out in a person's life.

- It focuses on verbally accessible memory and situationally accessible memory.

### B. Insight-Oriented Method

- Psychodynamic types tend to look at preexisting, unconscious methods that got overwhelmed through trauma.

- Hypnotherapy focuses on using a relaxed, hypnotic state to work out repressed material and integration of a traumatic event.

### C. Group Therapy

- This approach can occur in a number of different types of domains.

- It has several strengths, including the bonding that occurs in people that have experienced events, feedback, support, and security.

- Group therapy can be a helpful context as one part of restoring the person to wholeness.

## VI. Effective Treatment

### A. Tends to Address Two Core Domains:

- Memory

- Emotional regulation

### B. Involves

- Detailed, repeated exposure to traumatic information

- Modification of maladaptive beliefs about events, symptoms, and behaviors

## VII. Best Practice Guidelines

### A. Focus on screening and assessment.

- Defining clearly what the symptoms are, how it affects a person's life, and the resources available to a person is crucial for effective treatment.

- The counseling process is going to be painful for the person, and proper screening and assessment can be a helpful process to motivate them to move forward in effective counseling.

- Use a step-wise process and have a safety plan.

### B. Establish a pathway that makes sense and provide a rationale.

- Help the person have a sense of what the destination and direction is, and have a "here and now" focus.

- The counselor must have empathy and reflective listening skills, as well as the ability to be creative and flexible.

- The counselor should have a multidisciplinary, comprehensive approach.

### C. Remember that people are created in the image of God.

- Uniqueness (autonomy)

- Oneness (connection)

- Openness (influence)

## VIII. Conclusion

A. Romans 8:28-30 – *"And we know that for those who love God all things work together for good, for those who are called according to His purpose. For those whom He foreknew He also predestined to be conformed to the image of His Son, in order that He might be the firstborn among many brothers. And those whom He predestined He also called, and those whom He called He also justified, and those whom He justified He also glorified."*

B. Romans 8:35-39 – *"Who shall separate us from the love of Christ? Shall tribulation, or distress, or persecution, or famine, or nakedness, or danger, or sword? As it is written, 'For Your sake we are being killed all the day long; we are regarded as sheep to be slaughtered.' No, in all these things we are more than conquerors through Him who loved us. For I am sure that neither death nor life, nor angels nor rulers, nor things present nor things to come, nor powers, nor height nor depth, nor anything else in all creation, will be able to separate us from the love of God in Christ Jesus our Lord."*

C. Most people, particularly in the United States, experience traumatic events in their lives. The good news is that most people recover without the need for professional assistance. Recovery is possible and expected; people are resilient. Post-traumatic growth is astounding, because there is the potential that when people are shattered and their worldview falls apart, they find out they can be better than they were before. There is hope in the midst of suffering and separation.

## CCCT 305 Study Questions

1. Discuss the three symptom clusters, and give details regarding their implications to people dealing with PTSD.

2. What are the three basic treatment principles that counselors should use, regardless of the mode of therapy that is involved in treating the client?

3. Discuss cognitive-behavioral strategies.

4. What are the four classes of medications that Dr. Lyles discussed, and how can they help a person suffering from PTSD?

5. Discuss what is involved for effective treatment, regardless of type or combination.

# CCCT 306
# THE JOURNEY FROM TRAUMA TO TRANSFORMATION: A SOLDIER'S STORY

MG (Ret.) Bob Dees, Sgt. Gary Beikirch, M.A., & Lolly Beikirch

## Course Description

In this lesson, students will be exposed to the story of Sergeant Gary Beikirch, who received the Medal of Honor for his service in Vietnam. The Medal of Honor is the highest award for valor in action against an enemy force which can be bestowed upon anyone serving in the U.S. Armed Forces, and the deed for which it is awarded is to be one of personal bravery or self-sacrifice so conspicuous as to clearly distinguish the individual for gallantry above his comrades, and must involve risk of life. Gary Beikirch, along with his wife Lolly, shares his experiences of healing and restoration from combat-related PTSD, providing background information, as well as the reasons regarding why counseling is important to anyone suffering from trauma-related PTSD.

## Learning Objectives

By the end of this lesson, students:

1. Will be able to be exposed to a primary source story of a soldier who experienced combat trauma from the Vietnam War.

2. Will be able to reflect on the healing process that brought Gary Beikirch to a sense of restoration from PTSD.

3. Will be able to learn the Beikirchs' perspective on how to engage with PTSD sufferers of trauma, whether combat-related or not.

# I. Background Information

A. Date of Action: April 1, 1970, in Kontum Province, Vietnam

B. Sergeant Gary Beikirch was a medic with the Green Berets in a camp near Cambodia. Though he was wounded twice in an intense, devastating attack, he refused treatment and asked to be carried as he searched for others who were injured. When an incoming rocket came towards him, one of his 15-year-old friends shielded him from further injury, but lost his own life in the process.

C. After being airlifted by helicopter to a hospital, Sergeant Beikirch woke up in the hospital with a chaplain by his side, asking if he wanted to pray. After a year in the hospital, Beikirch returned to civilian life, became a Christian, and entered seminary, determined to return to Vietnam as a missionary.

D. The Vietnam War left him so emotionally scarred that he moved to a cave in New Hampshire and let his hair grow below his shoulders while pursuing his studies. When the military located him to let him know that he was a Medal of Honor recipient and to invite him to Washington for the presentation, things began to change.

E. Following the ceremony, Beikirch completed a seminary degree as well as a Masters in counseling. He decided that God wanted him to help children, and he worked as a school counselor in a Rochester middle school.

# II. Experiences Leading to Post-Traumatic Stress Disorder

A. Intensity of impact

- Did not have a stable home life as a child

- Special forces training helped self-confidence and gave the opportunity to expand creativeness and resourcefulness.

- Living with the people in Vietnam created the first real connection in developing meaningful relationships with people, especially the 15-year-old mountain boy who became a bodyguard.

- Symptoms of PTSD from these factors included guilt, nightmares, and rage.

## B. Death of a Friend

- Deyo was Beikirch's "battle buddy"; it was a friendship forged in combat.

- In Vietnam, it was very important to know who could and couldn't be trusted.

- The intensity of April 1st was different from all other days. There was much guilt and personal pain, because, as a medic, Beikirch considered it his job to take care of the people.

- After Beikirch was wounded, Deyo carried him around for hours so that Beikirch could service those being killed. Beikirch was shot three times, and Deyo was wounded as well.

- Finally, Deyo shielded Beikirch from an incoming rocket, and did not move after the rocket exploded. In battle, there was no time for rage or anger. However, for years after, his death triggered rage and guilt that took a long time to bring healing.

## C. Events in the Hospital

- Beikirch considers his worst battle moment a few days after April 1, laying in a hospital bed in an intensive care ward, listening at night to the sounds of groaning and people dying.

- It was the worst part by far to Beikirch because he found himself going unconscious three or four times himself, and he was trying to keep himself from dying, but his eyes would close anyway.

- Beikirch felt a fearful, helpless feeling because there is no power in death. It was the most traumatic experience of his life.

- Ecclesiastes 8:8 – *"No man has power to retain the spirit, or power over the day of death. There is no discharge from war, nor will wickedness deliver those who are given to it."*

- "Becoming a Green Beret was such a tremendous accomplishment for me and provided such a meaning and significance to my life that I had never felt before, but it didn't mean a thing when I was dying and trying not to die."

### D. Searching for God

- In the hospital, there was a chaplain who talked about prayer and helped Beikirch have an awareness that God was there and that He cared. The chaplain gave him a cross.

- Beikirch entered college, and switched his major to pre-med, still searching for that God that he knew was real.

- After four months of college, he was wearing a fatigue jacket and walked by a student union. Some students joked about Beikirch, and spit on him. Finally, he could not take the criticism anymore.

- Beikirch traveled to New England, searching for meaning in life, looking for a sense of purpose.

- His search led him to a friend who eventually shared Christ, and he got involved in a memory system of Scripture, learned more about God, enrolled in a seminary in Northern New Hampshire, but still had difficulty being around people. Beikirch knew that God had forgiven him, but he placed a barrier around people and kept them at a distance.

- Gary lived in a cave while going to seminary, but eventually received a letter from Lolly, who became his wife three months later.

### E. Lolly's View

- Lolly was in love, and she did not realize the significance of the issues her new husband was dealing with.

- When they moved to Maine, she realized that he had major issues, even though there was not a term for it such as PTSD.

- Gary, Lolly, and their two kids moved into a shack with no running water, electricity, or toilet facilities.

- Gary was an associate pastor at the time, going through his own healing process with no name for his battle, living in the woods with a reluctance of talking. It was a strain on an early marriage.

- Lolly knew that Gary loved her and that God wanted them to stay together. She could not rely on her own understanding of what was happening but had to cling to what God was saying about the marriage.

- Proverbs 3:5-6 – *"Trust in the Lord with all your heart and do not lean on your own understanding. In all your ways acknowledge Him, and He will make straight your paths."*

### F. Gary's Healing Process

- Coming to Christ and feeling the healing, renewing power of Christ in his life was a huge step in his healing process.

- Vietnam destroyed every aspect of his life, including behavior, thoughts, feelings, and values. Gary hated himself for some of the things he remembered himself doing in Vietnam, and felt that he could not forgive himself, leading to self-hate.

- Identifying his problem as Post-Traumatic Stress Disorder helped.

- God working with him and Lolly as a couple also furthered the healing process.

### G. Lolly's Healing Process

- The two biggest contributing factors to Lolly's healing process of secondary trauma were the sole dependency on the Word of God and the Holy Spirit as her Comforter.

- Gary went to the cave to fall in love with God, but found that he had to come out of the cave to love other people. He loved Lolly, but he was detached from the family.

- She encouraged Gary to fight the battle within himself.

## III. Becoming Counselors

A. **Gary entered graduate school to become a school counselor. He let down walls with a compassionate friend in school, which was a huge step for him.**

B. **Learning to have a ministry of presence was important for both Gary and Lolly. Learning to be there when people are ready and standing with them for the long haul can often require walking through the pain.**

C. **Working on their marriage, being a couple, and working together in ministry encouraged Gary and Lolly to become counselors together.**

## IV. Advice for Counselors Across America Engaging with PTSD Sufferers of Combat Trauma or Trauma in General

**A. Have a ministry of presence.**

**B. Be there to listen in an accepting, non-judgmental environment.**

**C. Share the grief and guilt.**

**D. Understand Romans 8:28** – *"And we know that for those who love God all things work together for good, for those who are called according to His purpose."*

**E. Understand that healing takes time.**

- Medication for the purpose of forgetting can mask the problem. Forgetting isn't getting better.

- Getting better is being able to cry. It is being able to open oneself up to someone and let that person become a part of one's life. It is being able to heal and take what's happened and turn it around to build strengths in life. Getting better is letting God turn things around.

**F. Know how one's church can reach out to the military.**

## V. Bottom Line to Counselors or Sufferers of Trauma

**A. Put Proverbs 3:5-6 into practice** – trust in the Lord and allow Him to direct one's paths.

**B. Understand that PTSD and its impact on behavior are very real. God's intervention can heal despite the biology.**

## CCCT 306 Study Questions

1. What stood out about Gary Beikirch's experiences on April 1, 1970 that probably led to his development of PTSD?

2. Discuss the behavioral changes that were evident in Gary's behavior after his release from the hospital and return to civilian life.

3. How was Lolly affected through secondary trauma of PTSD?

4. Discuss the healing process that was evident in Gary Beikirch's life.

5. What do Gary and Lolly Beikirch recommend to counselors who are engaging with PTSD sufferers of trauma?

# UNIT FOUR
# MILITARY APPLICATIONS

# CCCT 401
# WAR, DEADLY FORCE, AND THE BIBLE
## Todd Wagner, M.A.

## Course Description

War is a difficult topic to discuss, but people in all professions need to reconcile the requirements of their profession with the requirements of faith and biblical truth. This lesson addresses what God thinks about the military profession by discussing biblical references and moral dilemmas that soldiers often face. Todd Wagner will help students discover a biblical worldview that is consistent with the Scriptures regarding deadly force as it pertains to war.

## Learning Objectives

By the end of this lesson, students:

1. Will be able to apply Scripture to military scenarios.

2. Will be able to understand the principles of just war.

3. Will be able to understand a biblical worldview regarding the government's role in war.

I. **Reconciling a Soldier's Calling with the Commandment,** *"Thou Shalt Not Kill"*

    A. War is not what was, should be, or will be. War – the need for the restriction of evil – is what is.

    B. A soldier that does not fear the use of deadly force is a deadly soldier.

    C. War came as a result of the escalation of evil in man.

    D. Men can improve in almost everything, except morality.

    E. Genesis 9:6 – *"Whoever sheds the blood of man, by man shall his blood be shed, for God made man in His own image."*

    F. There will not be a "war to end all wars" until peace comes another way.

    G. Isaiah 2:4 – *"He shall judge between the nations, and shall decide disputes for many peoples; and they shall beat their swords into plowshares, and their spears into pruning hooks; nation shall not lift up sword against nation, neither shall they learn war anymore."*

    H. Revelation 21:4 – *"He will wipe away every tear from their eyes, and death shall be no more, neither shall there be mourning, nor crying, nor pain anymore, for the former things have passed away."*

    I. War is a divine right, privilege, and responsibility.

    J. To not war is to rebel, as well as warring unjustly.

    K. Romans 13:1-4 – *"Let every person be subject to the governing authorities. For there is no authority except from God, and those that exist have been instituted by God. Therefore whoever resists the authorities resists what God has appointed, and those who resist will incur judgment. For rulers are not a terror to good conduct, but to bad. Would you have no fear of the one who is in authority? Then do what is good, and you will receive his approval, for he is God's servant for your good. But if you do wrong, be afraid, for he does not bear the sword in vain. For he is the servant of God, an avenger who carries out God's wrath on the wrongdoer."*

L.  Government exists because men are evil.

M.  Peace only comes in the hearts of a people and societies through a relationship with the Prince of Peace.

N.  The idea that war is necessary is something Scripture affirms. Because of rebellion, governments need to be able to deal with evil men.

O.  Romans 3:10-18

P.  There are several institutions necessary for humankind to work – home, church, and government all have authority.

Q.  Micah 6:8 – *"He has told you, O man, what is good; and what does the Lord require of you but to do justice, and to love kindness, and to walk humbly with your God?"*

R.  When government decides not to fulfill its role, people suffer.

S.  Letting evil alone and trying to isolate evil does not work. Evil grows.

T.  Appeasement is a failed understanding of how to deal with evil.

U.  Proverbs 30:15 – *"The leech has two daughters: Give and Give. Three things are never satisfied; four never say, 'Enough'"*

## II. Words Helpers Can Give Individuals in the Military who are Suffering from Soul Trauma

A. God gives the sword to the state but not to the individual.

B. How the governments of the world are called to respond to abuse, wrong, and evil is different from how individual humans are called to respond.

C. Romans 12:14, 17, 21 – *"Bless those who persecute you; bless and do not curse them … Repay no one evil for evil, but give thought to do what is honorable in the sight of all … Do not be overcome by evil, but overcome evil with good."*

D. If a nation does not have a good judiciary, they will die from within. If they don't have a good military, they will die from without.

E. One can be a pacifist because of conscience, but cannot be a pacifist because of Christ.

F. God has ordained that government is to be a temporal restrainer of evil.

## III. Augustine's "Just War" Theory

A. God approves "just war," but He abhors imperialism.

B. Tenets of a Just War

- Legitimate authority

- Just cause

- Just intent

- Specific and achievable goals

- Proportionality in cost and response

- Intent to respond to the threat of aggression, not to vent anger associated with the enemy

- Take effort not to expand targets beyond military ones

## IV. Conclusion

A. God is not just concerned about macro justice, but also about individual justice.

B. God says that judgment always begins with His people.

C. Be part of the provision for soldiers in the execution of justice and in the recovery process that is unnatural to man.

D. Understand that part of government's responsibility is fulfilling its duty, and God will hold governments responsible who war unjustly or who do not war at all.

E. Counselors must comfort those who engage in selfless sacrifice, putting themselves at risk for an honorable and just cause.

## CCCT 401 Study Questions

1. Discuss the necessity of reconciling the requirements of any profession with the requirements of faith and biblical truth.

2. Discuss the principle of war existing as a result of the escalation of evil in man.

3. According to the presenter, what is the purpose of government and why does it exist?

4. Discuss the tenets and implications of Augustine's "Just War" Theory.

5. What role can counselors play in helping soldiers understand war from a biblical worldview?

# CCCT 402
# THE REALITIES OF MILITARY SERVICE ON THE SERVICE MEMBER
## Don Snider, Ph.D. & LTG Van Antwerp

## Course Description

Counselors and caregivers need to be exposed to the reality of military service and its impact on the service member. Each person is unique and possesses different dynamics that will influence their reactions to events. This lesson will teach students about demographics, reasons people enlist in the service, the issues regarding family members, deployment and redeployment, wounds of war, and how to deal with the death or loss of a service member. Overall, this lesson will help counselors be more effective by helping them understand these crucial factors.

## Learning Objectives

By the end of this lesson, students:

1. Will be able to learn about the difficulties of reintegrating into society following deployment.

2. Will be able to learn about family dynamics that accompany military life.

3. Will be able to better understand the challenges of a wounded warrior, and how the counseling community can help.

## I. Military Dynamics

A. **Citizen Soldier – People choose to move from being citizens to soldiers, but then they place their identity as soldiers in front of their identity as citizens. Reserve components are more citizen soldiers.**

B. **Everyone who enters the military has a concept of personal purpose and service.**

C. **Research from the early phases of the Iraq war is clearly documenting the positive incentive of mission on performance.**

D. **Meaning of intense wartime experience is found in the transcendent, and not having a connection to that transcendent meaning can interfere with finding meaning in a healthy way.**

E. **Two Greedy Institutions**

- Military sociologists describe two greedy institutions: the family and the military vocation.

- Both the family and the military vocation have intense demands.

- There need to be two things for these institutions to thrive:

  1) consistency in commitment and in action

  2) predictability in the short- and mid-term

- However, these institutions do not have those elements right now; they are intensely needy institutions.

F. **Identity of soldiers is important to understand because satisfaction of service keeps them on active duty.**

## II. The Wounded Warrior

A. Each individual warrior will have to construct and reconstruct meaning of personal identity on his/her own. In order to continue, they will have to reorient their identity significantly within the limitations they have.

B. Veterans' futures cannot – and should not – be detached from what they have done in the past.

C. They need around them that moral, caring community to help them, if necessary, bring closure to a part of their life that was very satisfying, draw those satisfactions from it, and move on to a new phase of life where they can find equally satisfying results.

## III. The Dynamic of Faith

A. In its broadest view, faith is an element that is an intertemporal dimension.

B. Faith creates expectations about the future, and in trauma situations, those expectations are challenged.

C. There is a faithful God, and the manifestation of His care here on earth is the church. In the church, people should be able to find the love and care that He will show as people find out what they are to do next for Him (service, not self).

D. Churches should display a very conscious commitment of older military veterans to become a part of the lives of younger veterans who are returning.

E. Networking within a faith community to veterans of different generations should not be overlooked.

F. There is an intense intersection between growing spirituality and higher education.

G. Repetitive deployments have deepened the desire and willingness to explore spiritual meaning.

H. The potential for spiritual growth and maturation for this "Generation Y" is tremendously untouched.

## IV. The Service Member

A. The majority of young people enter the military for educational benefits, but due to the training, there is a change that moves service members toward selfless service to country.

B. Characterizing the Sacrifice

- Self-effacing

- Wounds of war

- Impact on families

C. Family Dynamics

- About 50% of U.S. soldiers are married.

- About 50% of American soldiers come from military families.

D. Reflections on the Challenges of Wounded Warriors

- There is usually a soul-searching about what they personally did and what others did for them.

- Medications and memories may also be factors.

- Helpers can listen, put their arms around them, and pray with them.

E. There are differing responses to God when something traumatic happens, including elements of anger, guilt, false guilt, bitterness, and some do have a willingness to pray.

F. **National Guard/Reserve Forces**

- There is a difference when they come home, because they have different dynamics that take place in living in the community.

- How to help them return home as contributing citizens:

  1) Support groups are very important.

  2) A lot of service members find that the dynamics of their families have changed when they return from tours of duty.

  3) Isolation is one of the worst things; people need to reach out to the service members and support them.

  4) A church can be effective in the life of a returning warrior by allowing them to join up with others of similar experiences.

# V. Unseen Wounds of War

A. **People should build the relationship with service members before they deploy, or while they are deployed. It is difficult to come back and be in a totally foreign group, so this sort of outreach would inspire quicker integration into the community.**

B. **Unseen wounds are the challenges for the long-term.**

C. **Today, people have a better understanding of PTSD.**

D. **Reality of Death and Impact on a Service Member**

- Many young people think they are invincible. When that is shaken by the death of a friend, there is an additional burden. They will ask, "Why did it have to happen?"

- A great part of the solution is to find purpose that only God can help a person find.

- The soldiers should get back with their units as quickly as they can to get back in that purpose.

## VI. Guidance to Counselors within Churches on Dealing with Combat Trauma

### A. Before helping, be educated about the makeup of the soldier.

- They place the mission first, never accept defeat, never quit, and never leave a fallen comrade. These are the four pillars of soldiers.

- Being defeated in their minds causes them to search their souls and ask, "What could I have done differently?"

- Counselors need to understand the basic framework.

### B. Soldiers know how to be under authority. This means counselors can use a different approach with them.

### C. Take opportunities to go out and be physically engaged.

### D. Have soldiers be a part of something that is making a difference for others.

### E. Get them out where they can mingle, talk, and feel like a normal person.

### F. Be persistent, hang in there, and be there for the long haul so that soldiers continue to feel the support.

**CCCT 402 Study Questions**

1. Discuss the concept of the two greedy institutions. What can this mean for a military family on a practical level?

2. What are some of the dynamics and issues that a wounded warrior might face when returning home?

3. Discuss the element of faith, and how it is important in understanding a person's identity and purpose. How can this apply to the military?

4. What are some challenges that the National Guard and Reserve troops might face regarding reintegration into society after combat?

5. What can counselors and the church do to help service members and their families?

# CCCT 403
# THE REALITIES OF MILITARY LIFE FOR FAMILIES
## MG (Ret.) Bob Dees, LTG and Mrs. Van Antwerp,
## & Rosemarie Hughes, Ph.D.

## Course Description

In this lesson, students will gain a unique perspective from a panel discussing family life on the home front. There are unique challenges that military families will face, such as secondary trauma within the family, challenges of separation, the overall lifestyle and culture of the military, difficulties of deployment, homecoming realities, and the possibility of having a wounded soldier return home. This lesson will open students' eyes to the struggles that various military families can face and provide practical ways to provide encouragement for them.

## Learning Objectives

By the end of this lesson, students:

1. Will be able to understand some of the unique challenges posed on military family life.

2. Will have listened to Lieutenant General Robert Van Antwerp and wife Paula's personal story regarding family life in the military, which provides a personal perspective to students.

3. Will be able to gain insight on how a counselor can approach military families who are struggling.

## I. Four Main Areas of General Knowledge

### A. Military Culture and System

- No 40-hour work week.

- No entitled holidays.

- No choice of next duty station.

- Behavioral expectations. Military children are subject to different behavioral expectations and often higher standards than their peers.

- Military culture runs the family's life.

- The military does not take into account a child's needs when a service member is ordered to move.

- The way the parent remaining at home handles the deployment is the key to the child's well-being.

### B. Realities of Deployment

- Children have to adapt to a parent going away for a long time on a regular basis.

- Anxiety levels may increase that the service member return safely.

- The media may exacerbate the anxiety, especially within children.

- The spiral of deployment has grown, becoming longer and having a shorter turnaround time.

- Families are experiencing deployment fatigue.

- Technology is such that families can use email, video, and cell phones to stay in touch.

- The deployed parent should be kept psychologically present while physically absent.

- There are also possible problems of deployment.

    1) father remoteness & difficulty reintegrating

    2) child abuse (emotional or physical)

    3) emotional difficulties for child

    4) pre-deployment stress

    5) parentification of children

    6) home parent may become overwhelmed

    7) financial difficulty

## C. Homecoming

- Usually a happy occasion, but the child can be negatively affected.

- The reality is that being back with the family means there are spousal and family demands that did not have to be dealt with when deployed.

- It is important not to put unrealistic expectations on the first day or week back from deployment; reacquainting and reorientation needs to occur naturally.

- The couple needs to be flexible and adaptable, bringing resilience to the family.

## D. The Wounded Warrior

- In the current war in Iraq, there are more missing limbs and head injuries reported than in perhaps any other war besides the Civil War.

- This issue requires an unanticipated adaptation by spouses and children.

- There are long-range concerns as well.

    1) Family needs to be able to return to normal.

    2) The injured spouse will have the question of whether or not he/she will be able to return to the service.

3) the question of the availability of the military to care for needs

4) the possibility of the loss of income

5) An injured spouse will be unable to do what he/she used to because of new caregiving needs.

- If the service member returns with or develops PTSD, there is a strong chance of secondary traumatization of the spouse and children.

## II. Other Considerations

A. **The child's position in the family is important, because experiences can be different depending on the age of the child.**

B. **Retirement can also be an at-risk time for the family.**

## III. Internet Resources

- www.crumilitary.org

- www.militaryonesource.com

- www.militaryfamily.com

## IV. The Van Antwerps' Perspective

A. **Culture as an Army Family**

- Passionate about the contribution that troops make

- A unique bond that all people in the service have

- Cannot picture life outside the military

- Feel a commitment to do everything they can to help younger soldiers and families in ways that are difficult for them

## B. View of Young Military Family Challenges and Opportunities

- Young marrieds are taking challenges on with an unparalleled jointness.

- A young wife/husband of a soldier must take on the adventure of the other person.

- Society tends to focus on the negative, but it is a noble task; young husbands and wives standing behind their spouses is inspiring.

- "There's nothing harder than loving a soldier."

- *"Your eyes saw my unformed substance; in Your book were written, every one of them, the days that were formed for me, when as yet there was none of them. (Psalm 139:16)"*

- Re-entering the family can be a stressful time and can take months, especially if there is an inner wound within the soldier.

## C. Subject of Separation

- Desert Storm was a difficult deployment for the Van Antwerps.

- Communication is key; though the couple is separated physically, the soldier is not unapproachable.

- Make decisions jointly, and continue things that hold a family together.

- Regarding multiple deployments, try to take every deployment as a brand new adventure so there are not cumulative effects.

- Have purpose and hope on the home front.

## D. Wounds of War

- There is a seen and unseen impact on families.

- Generally, the soldier will vent frustration on a family member. In this scenario, stay close and supportive, but do not hover or take it personally.

- Part of the healing is recognizing where one can join in with someone who has had similar injuries.

- A big challenge is wondering what the soldier can do after the injury.

## E. Advice to Counselors

- Recognize that if a person is struggling, then the family could be struggling as well.

- If the head of the household is dragged down, then the rest of the household can be dragged down too.

- The trauma can be transferred to other members of the family.

- Bring others alongside the soldiers who have experienced the same types of things.

## F. To Those Wanting to Encourage Young Families

- Realize that there can be a tough early-married road with deployments and training times.

- Don't miss the lessons that can be learned through adversity.

- Families can become so strong through these difficulties.

- Looking at the other side of the tunnel can give strength.

- It is the family that ultimately makes the soldier strong.

## G. Nate Self's Story (Former Army Ranger)

## CCCT 403 Study Questions

1. Discuss the military culture and system, and how these challenges might affect a family.

2. What are some realities associated with deployment, and how could they affect children of a military family?

3. Discuss some of the challenges and opportunities that young military families are facing today.

4. What are some potential ways for a family to be affected if a soldier comes home from war wounded?

5. How can counselors reach out to soldiers and their families when they are facing difficult times?

# THE COMBAT TRAUMA SPECTRUM
Rev. Chris Adsit & Rev. Rahnella Adsit

## Course Description

The combat trauma spectrum does an excellent job of showing a point of pain and matching it up with the right intervention. During this lesson, students will learn from Chris and Rahnella Adsit as they give students the big picture regarding what combat trauma is and how it impacts the lives of many individuals. Understanding the combat trauma spectrum is the first step in treating the trauma, and students will become more knowledgeable in this area by the end of this lesson.

## Learning Objectives

By the end of this lesson, students:

1. Will be able to understand what combat trauma is and how it affects both the lives of individuals and also of their families.

2. Will be able to understand both the similarities and the differences in Acute Stress Disorder (ASD) and Post-Traumatic Stress Disorder (PTSD).

3. Will be able to evaluate the Combat Trauma Spectrum and learn how to effectively use it as a counseling tool.

## I. The "Big Picture" of Combat Trauma

A. **When a person is impacted by a traumatic event, the trauma's thumb print is etched on the person's body, soul, and spirit. This can affect a person's:**

- Will to live

- Beliefs about God

- Beliefs about himself

- Beliefs about the world

- Dignity

- Sense of security

B. **According to Veterans Affairs, 80% of Operation Enduring Freedom (OEF) or Operation Iraqi Freedom (OIF) troops acknowledge that they have serious mental health issues.**

C. **Combat trauma, or PTSD, has been called many names throughout the century, which makes it clear that this disorder is not unique to modern wars, but is common to all wars. It wasn't until 1980 that the American Psychiatric Association formally identified, named, and defined the results of an extreme traumatic experience as Post-Traumatic Stress Disorder.**

## II. What is Combat Trauma?

A. **Combat trauma involves the responses that a service member has to the various stresses of war.**

B. **Combat trauma can also be referred to as "Deployment-Related Stress."**

C. **Soldiers who return from deployment who were not directly involved in combat can still experience the same distressing symptoms as those who were directly involved.**

Adjustment Disorders

| Reactions to Stressors Increasing in Severity | First Month of Symptoms | Next Three Months | Beyond Three Months |
|---|---|---|---|

Combat/Operational Stress Reactions       Acute Stress Disorder        Post-Traumatic Stress Disorder

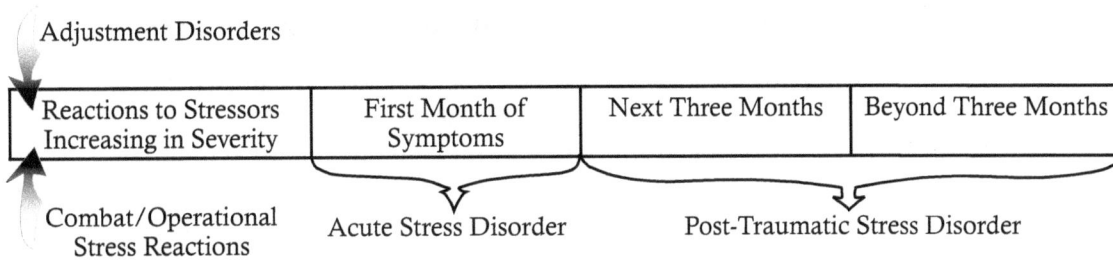

## III. Overview of the Combat Trauma Spectrum

### A. Pre-Deployment/Deployment/Reintegration Issues

- Among the mildest issues on the spectrum

- Certainly, still anxiety and adjustment issues

### B. Combat/Operational Stress Reactions

- These are normal reactions for anyone who goes into battle, and are not mental illnesses.

- Symptoms can appear like those of PTSD, Acute Stress Disorder, or adjustment disorders.

- Symptoms tend to occur immediately after a stressful event and people recover quickly without significant treatment.

### C. Adjustment Disorders

- These are much more common than Acute Stress Disorder or Post-Traumatic Stress Disorder.

- They are usually much less serious than ASD or PTSD.

- These can occur when an individual is exposed to identifiable stressors causing a reaction that results in significant excessive stress or impairment.

- The reaction can involve three symptoms: depression, anxiety, and/or disturbance of contact.

- Adjustment disorders can occur up to three months following an event, but they are usually resolved within six months.

IV. **Acute Stress Disorder and Post-Traumatic Stress Disorder**

    A. The main difference in Acute Stress Disorder and Post-Traumatic Stress Disorder is that Acute Stress Disorder encompasses an increased incidence of dissociative episodes, and a shortened onset and duration of symptoms.

    B. It is important to understand that physiologically, the lower brain always trumps the two halves of the upper brain.

    C. Sometimes people keep reliving the trauma because the brain stays stuck in the crisis alert mode.

    D. The shock of trauma physically alters parts of the brain.

    E. Three Symptom Categories of ASD and PTSD

- Re-experiencing symptoms

- Avoidance symptoms

- Arousal symptoms

V. **Andi Westfall's Story (Former Army Flight Medic)**

VI. **Stages of Combat Trauma**

    A. Acute Stress Disorder: Symptoms continue four weeks or less.

    B. Acute PTSD: Symptoms continue one-to-three months or less.

    C. Chronic PTSD: Symptoms persistent three months or more.

    D. Delayed Onset PTSD: Symptoms start six months or more after.

## VII. Post-Traumatic Stress Disorder

A. One can acquire PTSD through combat, natural disasters, accidents, kidnapping, torture, viewing any of the above, or receiving tragic news about self or others close to self.

B. Not everyone exposed to an event will experience PTSD, and only about 5 to 10% of non-combat individuals will experience PTSD.

C. **Factors that Contribute to an Individual Being Less Likely to Experience PTSD**

- Fewer, less intense events

- Attached meaning and significance to the event

- Mental and emotional state of the individual

- Belief in one's mission

- The individual's ability to envision the greater good

- Positive leadership

- Teamwork/support

- Debriefing within 72 hours

D. **Factors that Contribute to an Individual Being More Likely to Experience PTSD**

- Frequent, intense events

- Personal involvement

- One event occurring on top of other current stressors

- Traumatic events in childhood

- Strong feelings of responsibility

## VIII. The Effects of Deployment on Spouse / Children

A. When a husband or wife goes off to war, adjustments have to be made by the home-front spouse. He/she must assume both parental roles, do all household chores, bear many emotional burdens that cannot be shared with the other spouse, understand that various temptations are more accessible, and overall family logistics are harder to accommodate.

B. One of the most debilitating problems is how a returning soldier can affect his/her family with PTSD.

C. Secondary Traumatic Stress: the traumatizing, negative effect of the combat troop's condition on his or her spouse and children

## IX. Combat Trauma and How It Has Impacted Military Women

A. More than 182,000 women have served in Iraq and Afghanistan.

B. The war in Iraq has been called an "Equal Opportunity War."

C. According to Veterans Affairs, women diagnosed with PTSD accounted for 14% of the total 27,000 veterans treated for PTSD.

D. 20% of women seeking VA care since 2003 showed signs of Military Sexual Trauma (compared with 1% of men).

## X. Conclusion

A. God is the Healer.

B. People are not.

C. Nevertheless, God wants to partner with each individual to construct a healing environment.

D. Isaiah 32:2 – *"Each will be like a hiding place from the wind, a shelter from the storm, like streams of water in a dry place, like the shade of a great rock in a weary land."*

# XI. Resources

A. *The Combat Trauma Healing Manual* is designed for the returning troop suffering from combat trauma. It is recommended for use in a small group, but can also be used in self-study mode. (Available at www.crumilitary.org/store)

B. *When War Comes Home* is designed for the wives of combat veterans. (Available at www.crumilitary.org/store)

C. The Bridges to Healing children's books are written for children whose parents who may have combat trauma. The first two books have resources and suggestions for the parents: *My Hero's Home!!* for K-3rd grade, *Helping My Hero!!* for 4th-6th grade, *My Hero Hurts!!* for teens. (Available at www.crumilitary.org/store)

**CCCT 404 Study Questions**

1. Chris and Rahnella Adsit talked about traumas becoming etched on a person's soul. What areas of a person's life can trauma affect?

2. Discuss the three categories of issues that were discussed as related to the Combat Trauma Spectrum.

3. List some differences and similarities in Acute Stress Disorder and Post-Traumatic Stress Disorder.

4. What are some factors that can contribute to an individual being more or less likely to experience PTSD?

5. What are some effects of deployment on a soldier's spouse and children, and why should counselors carefully take these effects into account?

# CCCT 405
# MILITARY MEDICAL SYSTEM, VETERANS MEDICAL SYSTEM, AND RELATED ISSUES
## Leigh Bishop, M.D., M.A. & MG (Ret.) Ken Farmer, Jr., M.A.

## Course Description

This lesson will help students understand the Veteran's Affairs medical systems so that counselors can team with them as they partner with military veterans. The presenters will discuss the ecosystem for military, especially for the wounded warrior, and how important it is to provide care and compassion for families of soldiers as well as the soldiers. Students will learn about the hidden wounds of war, and how to take a holistic approach regarding treatment and help for soldiers.

## Learning Objectives

By the end of this lesson, students:

1. Will be able to learn a general overview for the military medical system.

2. Will be able to understand various factors that counselors need to take into consideration, such as family dynamics and the wounded warrior.

3. Will be able to learn how to look at these issues from a holistic approach.

## I.    The Ecosystem for Military

A.  The Military Medical System is a very complex combination of the direct system (military hospitals and clinics) and partnerships with private sector companies to augment care.

B.  There is much sophistication and technology in Iraq and Afghanistan regarding medical help.

C.  For injured soldiers, the journey goes from the battlefront to Germany and then to the most appropriate medical facility in the United States.

D.  Families of soldiers should be provided care and compassion as well.

E.  Pastoral counselors are one of the categories of Tri-Care Certifiable Providers.

F.  There seems to be a stigma of seeking healthcare, particularly behavioral healthcare.

G.  Combat counseling teams can be a part of deployable force, to provide Critical Incident debriefing, preventative care, and suicide prevention programs.

## II.   National Guard and Reserve Forces

A.  Guard and reservists are being deployed in an unprecedented fashion.

B.  It is different for them now because the frequency and duration they have been deployed is phenomenal.

C. **Both Congress and the Department of Defense have put in place advantages for them and their family members.**

- There are new programs of coverage in military health systems that specifically address the Tri-Care military benefit that aren't specifically around military clinics.

- Networks are being expanded to meet the needs of guardsmen and reservists away from military hospitals.

D. **The growth over the past few years has been particularly focused in the broad areas. Experts are always looking for gaps, needs, and opportunities to expand to meet the needs for people.**

## III. Hidden Wounds of War

A. **Comorbidity. Outwardly visible wounds can often have wounds that one cannot see. Treating them together is a necessary but complicated process.**

B. **Mark 12:30 –** *"And you shall love the Lord your God with all your heart and with all your soul and with all your mind and with all your strength."*

C. **Mark 12:30 addresses the emotional, spiritual, mental, and physical dimensions of a person, providing a holistic approach.**

D. **There is a direct role for faith in this process. From a faith-based perspective, God is the Healer.**

E. **How to Deal with a Wounded Warrior**

- Treat them like one would treat anyone else.

- Ask them to talk about their experiences and missions.

- It is acceptable to talk to wounded soldiers about their experiences, even their injuries.

## IV. Holistic Approach

A. The healing process does not end in the hospital; rather, there is a role for churches and other organizations to take part in – they play a key role in holistic healing.

B. Build trust with patients and their families. Then move on to other steps of connection, openness, and caregiving.

C. Faith contributes to resiliency.

## V. Transition into the VA System

A. Veterans Affairs Mission – "To care for him who shall have borne the battle, and for his widow, and his orphan." (Abraham Lincoln)

B. Those who are discharged from the military prior to retirement are generally eligible for health care through the VA System.

C. Those who retire from the military (or have a medical retirement) are generally eligible for medical care either in the military system or possibly in the VA.

D. Often, VA Medical Centers are affiliated with the finest medical schools in the country.

E. New Veterans

- OIF: Operation Iraqi Freedom

- OEF: Operation Enduring Freedom (Afghanistan)

- Veterans should first enroll in the system by visiting the nearest VA hospital.

- In an urgent need, returning soldiers should not let lack of enrollment stop them from seeking care.

- "Vet Centers" – Facilities dedicated to counseling and psychotherapy for veterans and their families.

- Returning Veteran's Medical Health Screen – Initial contact with psychologist or social worker for lengthy and extensive interviews regarding background, family, and medical history.

## VI. Veterans and PTSD

A. The signature injuries of today's era combat are Post-Traumatic Stress Disorder (PTSD) and Traumatic Brain Injuries (TBI).

B. A person grounded in faith is more able to make a rapid transition to recovery from PTSD.

C. It can be very difficult for returning soldiers to reconnect with people around them.

D. While the typical psychiatric care for veterans is outpatient, there are also opportunities for inpatient care.

E. VA helps veterans of many different generations.

F. The biggest obstacle among veterans for seeking mental health treatment is the fear of a perception of weakness or a detrimental effect on their careers.

- PTSD is not a weakness or character problem.

- PTSD is an illness.

## CCCT 405 Study Questions

1. Discuss the importance of the unprecedented deployment of National Guard and Reserve forces.

2. Is there a stigma regarding military seeking healthcare, particularly behavioral healthcare? Discuss.

3. How should one treat a wounded warrior?

4. What is the role of faith and the faith community regarding the healing process?

5. What should a new veteran do to initiate the process of becoming involved in VA healthcare services?

# CCCT 406
# ASSESSMENT AND TREATMENT PROTOCOLS
## Leigh Bishop, M.D., M.A. & Eric Scalise, Ph.D.

## Course Description

This lesson addresses assessment and treatment protocols in the military. Counselors can be challenged by troops coming back from war, because often the last thing on their minds is a mental health assessment. Students will learn the importance of teaming, partnership, and community. They will learn to view these issues through a wide lens, looking at the broad applicability of the treatment methodologies for the military in other practices that may not always relate to the military.

## Learning Objectives

By the end of this lesson, students:

1. Will be able to understand critical core issues of assessment.

2. Will be able to understand the importance of a team approach.

3. Will be able to learn different treatment protocols that can be used after assessment.

## I. Critical Core Issues of Assessment

A. Define specific, describable symptoms.

B. Consult with family members to get a complete picture.

C. Determine individual's progression over the trauma spectrum to determine intensity of treatment.

D. Get a sense of whether the individual might be a risk to him/herself.

## II. General Overview of Assessment

A. Accurate assessment of symptoms directs proper treatment.

B. The presence of certain specific symptoms may indicate Traumatic Brain Injury (TBI).

C. It is imperative to take a team approach.

D. Always assess potential for the presence of substance abuse.

E. Active, ongoing substance abuse will undermine treatment of PTSD.

F. Following thorough assessment, the treatment team should coordinate to plan the type and intensity of treatment required.

G. For individuals with intrusive symptoms, intensive psychotherapy will typically be recommended.

H.  Education about the illness is critical, both for the traumatized individual as well as their loved ones.

I.  Pre-deployment education can act as an emotional inoculation.

J.  Battlemind: Those habits of mind that one has to have to survive, and to help one's fellow service members survive, in the combat zone.

K.  Trauma can set into motion certain brain chemistry changes which are beyond any individual's will to control.

## III.  Treatment Protocols

A.  Medications are useful in treating all but the mildest cases of PTSD.

B.  **Common Medications**

- Celexa

- Prozac

- Wellbutrin

C.  Jesus acknowledged that the sick need a physician.

D.  The majority of medications used to treat PTSD are not addictive.

E.  Cognitive Behavioral Therapy is one of the most effective treatments available to sufferers of PTSD and other anxiety disorders.

F.  Cognitive Behavioral Therapy seeks to change bad habits of mind.

G. Having the support of a community is an important part of recovery.

H. The advantage of a faith community is that support is ongoing.

I. Mentalization – The ability of the patient not only to begin to have an appreciation of the mental processes in other people, but also to know that they are understood and empathized with by their caregivers.

J. Become educated about the necessary conditions.

K. Brain scanning, particularly SPECT scanning, can be useful for therapists. These scans show the brain's activity as opposed to anatomy.

L. Most psychological problems are not problems with the brain's anatomy, but rather problems with the brain's functioning.

## CCCT 406 Study Questions

1.  What are the four critical core issues of assessment discussed in the video?

2.  Discuss the importance of taking a team approach in assessment and treatment options.

3.  Why should one always assess for the presence of substance abuse?

4.  What is the role of medications in treatment?

5.  Discuss Cognitive Behavioral Therapy and its purpose in recovery.

# UNIT FIVE
# SPIRITUAL SOLUTIONS

# CCCT 501
# A THEOLOGY OF SUFFERING
Ron Hawkins, D.Min., Ed.D.

## Course Description

Throughout this lesson, Dr. Ron Hawkins helps students discover a theological basis for suffering. He addresses difficult issues such as the fallen nature of man versus the holy nature of God. Though God has a perfect plan for His children, all go through tribulation. Dr. Hawkins will reflect on suffering and help students place it in a proper perspective and context.

## Learning Objectives

By the end of this lesson, students:

1. Will be able to examine some reflections on the dynamics of suffering.

2. Will be able to gain a biblical understanding of suffering.

3. Will be able to see the hope that encompasses people, even in the midst of suffering.

# I. Reflections on Suffering

**A. Suffering produces crisis.**

**B. Suffering is universal.**

**C. Suffering involves the whole person.**

**D. Suffering is holistic in its impact.**

**E. Further Reflections**

- A quick fix does not work.

- A biblical foundation in the place of suffering – in the world and in the program of God – secures and anchors the helper.

- Ecclesiastes 1:15

- Job 14:1 – *"Man who is born of a woman is few of days and full of trouble."*

# II. A Biblical Understanding of Suffering

**A. Suffering has a beginning and an ending.**

**B. All endure suffering at some time.**

**C. People are created for shalom (peace) and suffering hurts them.**

**D. Suffering is never wasted in the divine agenda.**

**E. God suffers.**

F.  Suffering is inscrutable; people cannot make sense of it.

G.  Suffering is sometimes a ministry in a person's life to accomplish His objective.

H.  Suffering can be discipline for sin.

I.  Suffering may be the result of spiritual warfare or satanic attack.

J.  Suffering may be a tool to break one's love of the world.

K.  Suffering may be for the glory of God.

L.  Suffering may be the consequence of hurt in the family of origin.

M.  Suffering may be a part of filling up that which is lacking in the sufferings of Christ.

N.  Suffering can increase one's ability to connect with others who are suffering.

O.  Suffering may be connected to evil.

P.  Suffering may be caused by abandonment.

## III.  How Do Helpers Attend to Suffering People?

A.  First, gain biblical understanding.

B.  Commit to being very cautious.

C. Be a conduit for the calming grace of God.

D. Imitate the love and grace of God.

E. Accept their words.

F. Affirm their dignity and value.

## IV. Further Thoughts on Suffering

A. Though there is a chaos and purposelessness of suffering in the world, God, who is sovereign, can turn it to good.

B. Suffering provides the opportunity to be bitter or better, resting in God's faithfulness.

C. The loss of meaning is the doorway to death.

D. 2 Samuel 1:17-27

E. 1 Samuel 23

F. 2 Corinthians 12:7 – *"So to keep me from becoming conceited because of the surpassing greatness of the revelations, a thorn was given me in the flesh, a messenger of Satan to harass me, to keep me from becoming conceited."*

G. Ecclesiastes 1 and 3

H. Genesis 45:5

I.   Ecclesiastes 3:11

J.   2 Corinthians 1

K.   Ephesians 4:29 – *"Let no corrupting talk come out of your mouths, but only such as is good for building up, as fits the occasion, that it may give grace to those who hear."*

L.   Hosea 3

M.   1 Corinthians 10:13 – *"No temptation has overtaken you that is not common to man. God is faithful, and He will not let you be tempted beyond your ability, but with the temptation He will also provide the way of escape, that you may be able to endure it."*

N.   It takes a team – doctor, counselor, spiritual director, coach, family, friends – to minister to the total person.

O.   It's never too late or impossible. God can heal anything. There is indeed a message of hope.

## CCCT 501 Study Questions

1. Discuss the importance of developing a theology of suffering.

2. Dr. Hawkins states that "a biblical foundation in the place of suffering – in the world and in the program of God – secures and anchors the helper." What are your thoughts on this statement?

3. Discuss the points that Dr. Hawkins makes under "A Biblical Understanding of Suffering." Which of these stood out to you most, and why?

4. What Scripture references were integrated into the development of a theology of suffering? Did any stand out to you more than the others, and why?

5. How can helpers specifically attend to people who are suffering?

# CCCT 502
# THE ROLE OF THE CHAPLAIN
## BG (Ret.) Charlie Baldwin, M.Div., COL (Chaplain) Keith Ethridge, M.Div., & MG (Ret.) Bob Dees

## Course Description

A panel of presenters describes the role of the chaplain. Soldiers often look to chaplains as trusted commanders, who can help spiritual wounds, as well as hidden wounds of war and other trauma. Students will gain a better understanding of what a chaplain's job is, how they can influence soldiers, and learn some of the sensitive issues that chaplains deal with.

## Learning Objectives

By the end of this lesson, students:

1. Will be able to learn the background information about chaplains.

2. Will be able to understand the broader network of chaplains.

3. Will be able to understand specific roles of chaplains.

## I. What is a Chaplain All About?

A. Chaplains are constitutionally based.

B. Chaplains guarantee that servicemen and servicewomen can practice their faith overseas.

C. Chaplains are endorsed by denominations.

D. Chaplains require a masters degree and pastoral experience.

E. There are additional criteria to be a VA chaplain.

## II. Broader Network

A. Armed Forces Chaplain Board – A group consisting of the six active duty chaplain generals – the Chief of Chaplains and the Deputy Chief of Chaplains for the three services – as well as the reserve components (Guard and Reserves), who meet to advise the Secretary of Defense and the Joint Chiefs on matters of religious importance.

B. Veterans Community Outreach Initiative – A Veterans Affairs effort to partner with community clergy, faith-based organizations and parachurch organizations to help them counsel veterans effectively.

C. Local communities need to reach out to reserve veterans in need who may not have access to the help provided in the on-base community.

D. We must work through local churches and counselors to meet widespread needs.

## III. How Does a Chaplain Show Compassion?

A. **Help soldiers understand that combat stress is a natural human response.**

B. **Let service members know that God loves them and there is hope.**

C. **The ultimate answer is found in a personal relationship with Jesus Christ.**

D. **"Faith in the foxhole. Hope on the home front."**

E. **It is important to remember that chaplains are people who need to be ministered to also.**

- Compassion Fatigue – Trauma often hits chaplains "coming and going" and the stress on them can be overwhelming.

- Clergy education about the signs and symptoms of suicide helps prevent suicide.

- VA Suicide Prevention Hotline – 1-800-273-TALK (8155)

F. **Helping Families**

- Chaplains need to intentionally resist insensitivity to the needs of families around them.

- Army Family Covenant

- People in the community need to be sensitive to the reserve component and the difficulties that come with that unique military lifestyle.

G. **Dealing with Death**

- Do not be afraid to be involved.

- Being present matters, even when there is nothing to say.

- Help people turn pain into positive action.

## IV. Words of Wisdom for Counselors

A. Be present and aware of needs.


B. Pursue clinical training.


C. Walk with them through the valley of the shadow of death.


D. Pray that God might make one more alert to the needs.


E. Pray for boldness.


F. Invite a chaplain to come and speak at one's church or community event.

### CCCT 502 Study Questions

1. What does being a chaplain require?

2. Discuss the "broader network" of chaplaincy.

3. What are some of the ways a chaplain can show compassion?

4. How can chaplains help families?

5. If soldiers have great chaplains, is there still a need for community support?

# CCCT 503
# THE ROLE OF THE FAMILY AS A PLATFORM FOR SPIRITUAL HEALING
### Dennis Rainey, M.A.

## Course Description

The family is also part of the caregiving equation, and counselors need to understand their important role. In this lesson, Dennis Rainey will discuss God's plan and tools for marriage, and will provide encouragement to people who have difficult situations within their family settings. He will also discuss how families can be victorious and overcome traumatic scenarios by the grace and power of God.

## Learning Objectives

By the end of this lesson, students:

1. Will be able to learn how to build a spiritually strong marriage and family.

2. Will be able to learn practical application for growing a spiritually strong marriage.

3. Will be able to learn about the specific application for military families, who are facing increasing challenges.

## I. Military Families

**A.** Military families today are facing increasing challenges.

**B.** Military families have a tremendous amount of pressure on them because of war, and as a result many have unhealthy relationships and need practical help and hope.

**C.** Military divorce rates are up 28% among enlisted and 78% amongst officers (NBC News).

**D.** Matthew 7:24-27

## II. How to Build a Spiritually Strong Marriage and Family

**A.** Build according to the Master's blueprint.

**B.** Reject isolation and build oneness.

- Isolation is the enemy of every spiritually strong marriage and family.

- The natural tendency in marriage is not toward oneness, but toward isolation.

- Genesis 2:24-25 – *"Therefore a man shall leave his father and his mother and hold fast to his wife, and they shall become one flesh. And the man and his wife were both naked and were not ashamed."*

- Leave, cleave, receive – and in doing so, reject isolation.

**C.** Resolve conflict when it occurs.

- Ephesians 4:31-32 – *"Let all bitterness and wrath and anger and clamor and slander be put away from you, along with all malice. Be kind to one another, tenderhearted, forgiving one another, as God in Christ forgave you."*

- Forgiveness is giving up the right to punish.

- Spiritual discipline: Pray together every day.

### D. Remember Who the Enemy is.

- Marriage does not take place on a romantic balcony, but on a spiritual battlefield.

- Know the enemy in his primary tactics.

- Ephesians 6:12 – *"For we do not wrestle against flesh and blood, but against the rulers, against the authorities, against the cosmic powers over this present darkness, against the spiritual forces of evil in the heavenly places."*

- One's mate is never the enemy.

### E. Make a Courageous Commitment

## III. Three Applications for Growing a Spiritually Strong Marriage

### A. Guard One's Heart (Proverbs 4:23).

### B. Surround oneself with the right kind of influences.

- 1 Corinthians 15:33

- Be the right kind of influence to others.

### C. Invest in one's marriage regularly.

## CCCT 503 Study Questions

1. Discuss what Dennis Rainey meant when he talked about "who will be the builder of one's home?"

2. Discuss the role of isolation in a marriage relationship.

3. Who is the enemy, and why is this important to keep in mind in a marriage?

4. What are some practical applications for growing a spiritually strong marriage that were referenced in the video?

5. Discuss some military applications to this lesson.

# CCCT 504
# THE ROLE OF THE CHURCH AND THE PARACHURCH
## Neil Rhodes, B.A., Bill Butler, & MG (Ret.) Bob Dees

## Course Description

This lesson discusses the importance of the church being involved in the lives of trauma sufferers, as well as the necessity of teamwork and partnering with parachurch organizations. The presenters will discuss different programs, and how to team so that churches can have the best impact on the targeted population. Students will gain insight on the power of the local church to reach into the grassroots of America, partnering with the parachurch, in order to effectively help trauma sufferers.

## Learning Objectives

By the end of this lesson, students:

1. Will be able to learn key aspects that churches can do to reach out to the community.

2. Will be able to learn from the example of the Times Square Church in New York City.

3. Will be able to learn the effectiveness of parachurch organizations.

## I. How the Church Can Effectively Help Trauma Sufferers

A. Have a heart to reach out.

B. Be military friendly.

C. Reach out to the deployed.

D. Encourage and support special recognition services and events.

E. Understand that God can challenge churches with one veteran.

F. Be faithful – have love and appreciation.

G. Understand that key leaders are passion and desire.

H. Get started – love one veteran.

I. Provide consistent care, love, and talk.

J. Have a heart of compassion.

- It takes time to heal and reintegrate.

- It takes time to build/rebuild trust.

- Train to communicate, and learn how to love correctly.

K. **How to Minister to the Military**

- Isaiah 61

- Luke 4

## II. How the Parachurch Can Help

A. **An effective church should hold their mission with a loose grip, and understand that there are others who are important in meeting the needs of trauma sufferers.**

B. **Characteristics of Parachurch Organizations**

- Typically, Protestant and Evangelical

- Some cater to a defined spectrum of evangelical beliefs

- Most are self-consciously interdenominational or ecumenical

- Vehicles by which faith groups work collaboratively outside of and across denominations to engage with the world in social welfare and evangelism

C. **A parachurch organization can often dive deeply into the cultural context in which they are ministering.**

D. **A parachurch organization can provide focused, broad-reaching resources.**

E. **Parachurch organizations are part of the healing equation.**

F. **Parachurch organizations can act as a bridge between other organizations.**

G. **The most relevant felt need in today's armed forces is the impact of combat trauma.**

**H. Bridges to Healing Ministry**

- Seeks to mobilize churches

- *The E-Kit Video Seminar: Engaging the Military Community in Your Midst*

- *Combat Trauma Healing Manual*

- *When War Comes Home Manual*

- Bridges to Healing children's book series

**I. A Perfect Storm**

- People are recognizing a growing need for counseling services.

- There is a growing acceptance in culture that counseling help is relevant.

- There is an increasing shortage of providers, which is exacerbated by the fact that America is a nation at war.

## CCCT 504 Study Questions

1. Discuss ways that a church can begin reaching out to trauma sufferers.

2. Discuss how to begin having a heart of compassion.

3. What are parachurch organizations, and how can they complement the church's outreach?

4. Discuss some of the characteristics of a parachurch organization.

5. How can counselors take advantage of the role of the church and parachurch in the community?

# CCCT 505
# THE ROLE OF THE COUNSELOR AND THE COMMUNITY
## Linda Mintle, Ph.D.

## Course Description

Dr. Mintle gives students an overview of the mental health profession in order to help students learn when and how to give proper referrals. Identifying and connecting with these resources is crucial when working with victims of trauma. This lesson will also provide students with specific insights dealing with military families, and it will offer biblically-based thoughts about how the role of the counselor and the community is consistent with faith, values, and the Christian worldview.

## Learning Objectives

By the end of this lesson, students:

1.  Will be able to understand the various mental health disciplines.

2.  Will be able to learn about community service programs that are available.

3.  Will be able to learn how to properly choose a therapist for a particular trauma situation.

## I. Reports from the Pentagon's Task Force on Mental Health

A. There are significant gaps in the continuum of care for mental health.

B. There is a stigma attached to receiving mental health services.

C. The number of active duty mental health professionals is insufficient and likely to decrease without substantial intervention.

D. The network mental health benefit is hindered by fragmented rules and policies, inadequate oversight, and insufficient reimbursement.

## II. Understanding Mental Health Disciplines

A. Psychotherapist: A mental health professional who doesn't have any connection to licensing.

B. Psychoanalyst: A mental health professional who typically has a great deal of specific training to handle deep mental health issues.

C. Medical Doctor

- Can be Doctor of Medicine (M.D.) or Doctor of Osteopathy (D.O.)

- Major difference is that D.O.'s have additional training in physical manipulation techniques that are somewhat similar to chiropractic.

- Most doctors typically specialize in an area.

- Look for someone who is board certified.

- Psychiatrists prescribe medications; find out whether the psychiatrist does medication evaluations and follow up, or also psychotherapy.

### D. Psychologists (Ph.D. or Psy.D.)

- Ph.D. is a Doctorate of Philosophy with specialty in psychology and research.

- Psy.D. is a Doctorate of Psychology with an emphasis on clinical psychology.

- They are both licensed psychologists.

- They may prescribe medication in New Mexico and Louisiana.

- They typically operate in an area of specialty.

### E. Education Specialist (Ed.S.)

- Typically operate as a school psychologist

### F. Masters Level Psychologists

- Industrial and organization settings

- M.Ed. work as Licensed Professional Counselor.

### G. Social Workers

- Doctor of Social Work (D.S.W.)

- Master of Social Work (M.S.W.)

- Licensed as

  1) Clinical Social Worker (LCSW)

  2) Independent Clinical Social Worker (LICSW)

- Do not prescribe medication

### H. Mental Health Counselors

- Have a Masters Degree and several years of supervised experience

- Licensed as:

  1) Licensed Professional Counselor (LPC)

  2) Licensed Mental Health Counselor (LMHC)

## I. Marriage and Family Therapists

- Have masters or doctorate degrees

- Licensed as Licensed Marriage and Family Therapist (LMFT) or are members of the American Association of Marriage and Family Therapists (AAMFT)

## J. Pastoral Counselors (M.Div., D.Min., Th.D., D.Div.)

- Trained as mental health providers

- Work specifically with religious and spiritual aspects

- Licensing varies by state: AR, KY, ME, NH, NC, TN license pastoral counselors.

## K. Psychiatric Nurses (RN)

- Clinical Nurse Specialist

- Advanced Practice Registered Nurse (Masters Degree in Psychiatric Mental Health Nursing)

## L. Certifications

- CSAC: Certified Substance Abuse Counselor

- CAC: Certified Alcoholism Counselor

## M. www.MilitaryMentalHealth.org – a website designed to help people assess their mental health on a voluntary and anonymous basis.

## III. Community Services

    A. Substance Abuse Programs

    B. Emergency/Crisis Programs

    C. Domestic Violence Programs

    D. Mental Health Centers

    E. Child and Family Service Programs

    F. Consumer Credit Counseling Services

    G. Crisis Hotlines/Emergency Care

    H. Community Support Programs

    I. Church Support Programs

    J. One suggestion is to provide seminars for military groups.

## IV. Finding a Mental Health Provider

    A. Talk to health care providers.

    B. Word of Mouth

C. Check phone listings.

D. Ask health insurance companies.

E. Check spouse's employee assistance program.

F. Use a referral service from a National Professional Organization like the AACC.

G. Go to the chaplain.

H. Find a Family Service Center.

## V. Choosing a Mental Health Therapist

A. How severe are the symptoms?

B. Are there going to be medical needs?

C. What is the provider's level of expertise?

D. Will the provider accept TriCare insurance or provide help pro bono?

E. Considerations for Referrals

- Gender

- Age/generation

- Religion/faith

- Language/culture

- Office hours, fees, session length

- Treatment approach

- Area of specialization

**F. Does one need a Christian therapist?**

- The worldview of a therapist makes a big impact when dealing with traumas.

- Therapy is not "value-free."

- A Christian therapist facilitates people to the One True Healer.

- "Spiritual" does not mean Christian. Be certain what "spiritual" means before referring.

## CCCT 505 Study Questions

1. Discuss the significance of the report from the Pentagon's Task Force regarding mental health.

2. Briefly list and explain the different mental health disciplines.

3. What are some examples of community service programs that can benefit the community with their mental health services?

4. What are some ways that one can find an appropriate mental health provider?

5. Discuss the implications of choosing or not choosing a Christian therapist.

# CCCT 506
# FROM TRAUMA TO TRANSFORMATION:
# A TEAM APPROACH

Tim Clinton, Ed.D., MG (Ret.) Bob Dees, & Diane Langberg, Ph.D.

## Course Description

This final lesson ties the series together by giving final advice and comments from Dr. Tim Clinton, Major General Bob Dees, and Dr. Diane Langberg. Students will be able to serve the Lord together on behalf of trauma sufferers around the world by understanding the importance of the critical role of Jesus Christ in transforming a person. There is a pathway from trauma to transformation, and students will be better equipped to help trauma sufferers cross a bridge to healing.

## Learning Objectives

By the end of this lesson, students:

1. Will be able to review habits that foster resiliency in a trauma sufferer.

2. Will be able to learn applicable Scripture verses that deal with healing.

3. Will be able to understand the role of Jesus Christ in transforming a trauma sufferer's life.

## I. Scriptures that are Relevant to Helping Trauma Sufferers

A. 2 Timothy 4:7 – *"I have fought the good fight, I have finished the race, I have kept the faith."*

B. John 16:33 – *"I have said these things to you, that in Me you may have peace. In the world you will have tribulation. But take heart; I have overcome the world."*

C. Romans 8:28 – *"And we know that for those who love God all things work together for good, for those who are called according to His purpose."*

D. Romans 8:18 – *"For I consider that the sufferings of this present time are not worth comparing with the glory that is to be revealed to us."*

E. 1 John 5:19

F. Exodus 15:26

G. John 21

H. Proverbs 14:12

I. James 1

## II. Additional Points to Emphasize

A. Trauma is extreme, but sadly it is not unusual.

B. There are many different types of abuse and experiences of grief.

C. The military analogy is broadly applicable across many forms of trauma.

D. A person's core relational beliefs impact how he/she does, or doesn't do, relationships in life.

E. For clinicians, becoming educated about trauma and healing helps fill the gap between education and experience.

F. Healthy Habits to Foster Resiliency

- Make connections.

- Resist the temptation to judge those who lack resiliency.

- Have hope in Christ.

- Faith contributes to resiliency.

G. Caregivers must remember their frailty.

H. Self-care is paramount to endure.

I. Count the cost: Working with trauma on a daily basis will change a clinician.

J. Beware of the Messiah Complex: it is not the clinician's job to save the world.

K. The first cost of the caregiver is not the needs of other people, but their own personal love and obedience to Jesus Christ.

L. The ultimate example is Christ as traumatized Savior.

M. If all one has is knowledge and skill, it is helpful, but empty in and of itself. The great hope is in one's relationship with Jesus Christ.

N. 2 Corinthians 4:16-18 – *"So we do not lose heart. Though our outer self is wasting away, our inner self is being renewed day by day. For this light momentary affliction is preparing for us an eternal weight of glory beyond all comparison, as we look not to the things that are seen but to the things that are unseen. For the things that are seen are transient, but the things that are unseen are eternal."*

## CCCT 506 Study Questions

1. The presenters say that there are many different types of abuse and experiences of grief. What implications do these facts have for clinicians?

2. What Scriptures stood out the most to one personally?

3. Discuss some healthy habits that can foster resiliency, and why it is important for counselors to understand these habits.

4. What is the Messiah Complex?

5. What kind of costs do clinicians need to take into account when deciding whether or not to work with trauma on a daily basis?

www.ingramcontent.com/pod-product-compliance
Lightning Source LLC
Chambersburg PA
CBHW080610270326

41928CB00016B/2989